women's work

Los Angeles Homecare Workers
Revitalize the Labor Movement

Edited by Lola Smallwood Cuevas, Kent Wong, and Linda Delp

UCLA Center for Labor Research and Education

Los Angeles, California

2009

Contents

This book is dedicated to the memory of the founding leaders
of the Los Angeles homecare movement who are no longer with us.
Their sacrifice and determination will never be forgotten.

REV. JOE HARDWICK

CLAUDIA JOHNSON

BERT MACLEECH

MAY PARKER

FRANK STREETER

Acknowledgments

Women's Work: Los Angeles Homecare Workers Revitalize the Labor Movement is the result of a six-year labor of love that would not have been possible without the dedication and hard work of the homecare union activists and students who, over the years, wanted to see this historic campaign documented and recognized. The UCLA Labor Center would like to thank the Service Employees International Union United Long-Term Care Workers' Union Local 6434 for their support and their efforts to assist us in collecting the necessary documents, photos, and interviews for this publication. We are especially grateful to the SEIU staff and leaders, both past and present, who participated in hours of interviews so that we could document this important chapter of Los Angeles' social justice history. These union members also patiently participated in a series of photo sessions and helped with fact-checking, making this publication possible.

Historic photographs and campaign materials represent a major component of this book. Our thanks to Michael Minedeo, SEIU-ULTCW communications director, and Leigh Shelton, SEIU-ULTCW communication specialist, who scoured archives and hard drives to find these illustrations. We want to recognize leaders of the Los Angeles homecare movement, including Verdia Daniels, Laurene Mackey, Addie Parsons, and Shirley Leonard, who trusted us with their personal keepsakes from the 1999 victory for many months. The input and support of John Ronches and Wyatt Closs were invaluable. The consultation and access provided by Loretta Stevens, California Homecare Council director, allowed us to capture the voices of homecare workers and provided extraordinary editorial guidance throughout the project. We are also indebted to Loretta Williams and Amanda Figueroa for helping us collect and identify the many images of the homecare movement that make this book come alive.

We thank all the groups, organizations, leaders, and communities who have supported the production of this publication. We extend special thanks to Antonio Villaraigosa, mayor of Los Angeles; Andy Stern, SEIU president; Gerry Hudson, SEIU International executive vice president; Gray Davis, former governor of California; Rod Wright and Gwen Moore, former California state assembly members; Los Angeles County Board of Supervisor Mark Ridley-Thomas; Rev. James Lawson; and Rev. Cecil Murray.

This book reflects a twenty-three year struggle. It is impossible to capture all the voices and note all the contributions of everyone involved. However, we would like to acknowledge four unsung heroes of the Los Angeles homecare story: Pauline Strong, homecare provider and member organizer; Patricia Robinson, homecare provider and activist member; Rev. Carl Washington, former assemblyman for the 57th district; and Mike Woo, former Los Angeles city councilman.

Lastly, we are thankful for the amazing work of Lanita Morris and Joaquin Calderon, UCLA Downtown Labor Center project coordinators. Thank you for consistently delivering the key interviews, photographs, and research that ensure that so many voices are heard.

Thank you as well to all the UCLA Labor Center interns and work study students. Rachel Schley began the arduous task of collecting and compiling photographs and completing hours of transcription. Natalia Garcia's work during the final phases of the book turned countless files into a wonderfully organized manuscript. Elia Madera and Laura Accecia completed the final captions and provided final editing and design support.

Lola Smallwood Cuevas, project director of the UCLA Center for Labor Research and Education.

Kent Wong, director of the UCLA Center for Labor Research and Education.

Linda Delp, director of the UCLA Labor Occupational Safety and Health Program.

Preface

SEIU members gather around Sheryl Hubben during the budget rally in front of the Ronald Reagan State Building in Los Angeles on February 13, 2009. Ms. Hubben, who has been a homecare worker for over twenty years, explains how the workers and consumers she works with will be affected by budget cuts.

Kent Wong and Lola Smallwood Cuevas

In 1999 the American labor movement won its largest organizing victory in the past half-century when 74,000 homecare workers joined the Service Employees International Union (SEIU) in Los Angeles. Their victory represents the best of what the American labor movement has to offer millions of low-wage workers. This book documents the stories of the individuals responsible for the Los Angeles County homecare organizing campaign, evaluates its broader impact on the U.S. labor movement, and explains how a group of low-wage women, mainly women of color and immigrants, mounted a twelve-year campaign that would forever change their working conditions and their lives. The 1999 victory in Los Angeles also encouraged tens of thousands of homecare workers around the country to unionize. In California alone, the United Long-Term Care Workers' Union is now the largest in the state, with more than two hundred thousand members.

Considered "invisible workers" by many, homecare workers care for the elderly, disabled, and sick who require in-home assistance. The work of homecare encompasses a wide range of services, including bathing and feeding clients, taking them to and from medical appointments, monitoring medication, assisting with grocery shopping and cooking, and careful supervision to provide care to those with mental or physical illnesses.

Today homecare workers assist about 500,000 elderly and disabled persons throughout California. The state currently has the largest senior population in the nation, with more than 3.5 million people over age sixty-five. There are more than 300,000 homecare workers statewide. In the next ten years, the number of Californians requiring care will more than double. In 2011 the first of the baby-boomer generation will turn sixty-five and will qualify for federal and state programs for the elderly. This development will intensify the debate on homecare in America and on how to care for our elderly.

Historically this work has most often been done by female family members without pay or by women hired at low pay. Homecare has been undervalued and rarely recognized as a career, or even a real job. As a result of the stigma attached to homecare, many women are ashamed to admit that they are homecare workers.

These conditions began to change in 1962 when the Public Welfare Amendments Act, the Older Americans Act, and Medicare and Medicaid provided entitlements for support services at home. The entitlements were expanded in California in 1973 when Ronald Reagan created In-Home Supportive Services (IHSS) to enable low-income seniors and people living with mental and physical disabilities to live independently in their homes. California's homecare program was created as a consumer-directed program that recognizes each recipient's right to hire, train, and, if necessary, terminate his or her homecare worker, subject to approval by a social worker.

Since the 1980s, homecare has emerged as one of the fastest growing occupations in the health care industry, fueled in part by welfare reforms that increased the number of poor women moving from public assistance to the workforce. Homecare workers play an indispensable role in the health care delivery system in this country because without their essential care, most homecare clients would require institutionalization at public expense. Despite this crucial contribution, homecare workers have earned poverty wages, have had virtually no workplace protections or control over their working conditions, and, ironically, have not received health care benefits for their work.

In the 1980s, a small, determined group of mostly African American women joined forces with the SEIU. Ophelia McFadden, a pioneering African American leader within the SEIU, was the leading champion of this campaign. The innovative strategies used in this struggle introduced a new way of organizing that reshaped the relationship between unions and community and highlighted the leadership role that worker institutions must play in defining social policy and agendas.

Most major union organizing victories of decades past involved thousands of workers who worked in the same factory or at the same workplace, such as a large auto or steel plant. Even public-sector organizing campaigns involved government workers or teachers working in the same institutions. The unique challenge for homecare was to organize 74,000 workers in 74,000 different workplaces. Clearly, nontraditional organizing methods were required. The homecare organizers embraced community-based organizing strategies by identifying homecare workers block by block, neighborhood by neighborhood.

The organizers also developed a comprehensive political strategy to exercise the collective power and influence of homecare workers years before they gained union recognition. Their major legal hurdle involved the prior classification of homecare workers as independent contractors who were thus ineligible for union protection. The political mobilization strategy was essential to pressure elected officials from both the State of California and Los Angles County to ultimately recognize homecare workers as workers and to establish a Public Authority that would serve as the employer of record to negotiate with them.

The homecare workers also developed community allies, most notably with leaders of the disability rights movement, who were integral players as the primary clients of homecare workers. Together with the disability community, homecare workers formed coalitions to fight for funding for vital social-service programs. They also reached out to religious leaders and community organizations and promoted a vision of social justice through their campaign.

The lessons from the homecare victory extend to the broader labor movement, especially in this time of declining union density throughout the nation. Unions must challenge themselves to rethink organizing and organizing strategies. With the shift from a manufacturing economy to a service economy, unions must consider new ways of organizing workers in nontraditional occupations and in workplaces that historically have not been organized. Homecare workers have pioneered strategies necessary for the labor movement to maintain its presence as a relevant force for social justice in the twenty-first century.

This book is a tribute to those extraordinary leaders, a group of predominantly low-wage women of color, who persevered through many years to achieve this unprecedented victory. In the process they changed the course of labor history in Los Angeles and the face of the labor movement. The homecare organizing victory ensured that homecare workers would be invisible no more.

The UCLA Labor Center is especially pleased to publish this book because of our long-standing relationship with the United Long-Term Care Workers' Union. We have partnered with the union on the Homecare Worker Training Program, which has given thousands of homecare workers the opportunity to upgrade their skills and enter a career track for advancement. The 2000–2001 Community Scholars Program, sponsored by the UCLA Labor Center and the UCLA Department of Urban Planning, brought together labor and community leaders and UCLA graduate students; they focused on homecare, identifying the housing, transportation, and job development needs of the workers. In addition, many homecare workers have participated in UCLA Labor Center leadership schools and have risen to positions of significant leadership within their organizations.

Barack Obama and the Importance of Homecare

D uring the 2008 campaign, SEIU sponsored "Walk a Day in My Shoes," asking candidates for local, state, and national offices to experience the lives of SEIU members before candidates asked for the union's support in the voting booth. In August, presidential candidate Barack Obama spent the day with Pauline Beck, a homecare worker from Alameda County. He had breakfast with Ms. Beck and her family, and then he and Ms. Beck went to the home of her client, John Thorton. Senator Obama worked alongside Ms. Beck, providing the daily care that allows Mr. Thorton to remain at home.

"Change is building an economy that rewards not just wealth but the work and workers who create it. It's understanding that the struggles facing working families can't be solved by spending billions of dollars on more tax breaks for big corporations and wealthy CEOs. . . . Make sure that health care providers are properly compensated and have decent working conditions, that's what change is. I learned some specific things about the struggles that homecare workers are going through. . . . I think it makes all the difference to have a union represent someone like Pauline. . . . She described what it was like before SEIU reached out to her. She was getting paid a minimum wage and she didn't have health care benefits. Now as consequences to the work that SEIU has done, she's got a wage that pays ten dollars and change an hour, she's got health care—but there is still more work to be done."

— Presidential candidate Barack Obama speaking to SEIU members and leaders during the SEIU convention in Puerto Rico, June 2008

Campaign poster made by SEIU in August 2008 for Barack Obama's presidential candidacy.

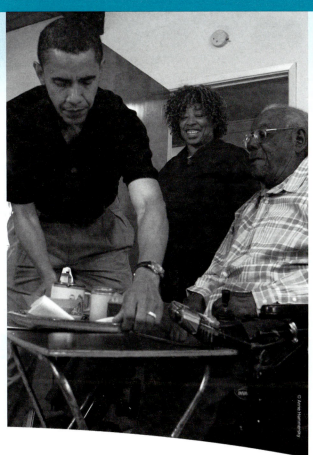

Dear Mr. President,

I am Pauline Beck – the California home care worker you spent a day on the job with in August 2007. You helped me provide care to Mr. John Thornton, an 86-year old man in a wheelchair who is able to stay in his home because of the care I provide.

I know you are very busy, but Mr. John and I, and my fellow home care workers and their clients, need your help.

You see, Governor Schwarzenegger wants to cut my pay back to $8 an hour. These are tough times, but if my pay gets cut to minimum wage I won't be able to support my family.

It's just wrong to pay us so little for taking care of people who have given our communities and our country so much.

Besides cutting my pay, the Governor also wants to cut the hours of care, even though people like Mr. John count on those hours to be able to stay at home. It makes no sense, Mr. President, because this will mean a lot of people will have to go into nursing homes that cost taxpayers a lot more.

Mr. President, I had hoped your stimulus bill, which is bringing billions of dollars to California, would help protect home care. Unfortunately, it seems that the money is being used for other things.

I understand that these are challenging times, but these cuts hurt California. They put vulnerable residents at risk of losing their independence and force hard working people like me into poverty.

I know you are a good man and I am proud of the job you are doing. I hope you and the Governor can work together to help Mr. John, me and the 750,000 of Californians just like us. It would make such a difference in our lives. Thank you.

SEIU launched its "Stop the Cuts" campaign in the spring of 2009 in response to California Governor Arnold Schwarzenegger's proposal to roll back pay for homecare workers to minimum wage as a way of solving the state's fiscal problems. The campaign included tens of thousands of letters, emails, and petitions to local and state representatives. An avalanche of demonstrations, rallies, and discussions were held in Sacramento and across the state, including a rally in Los Angeles that was attended by more than 5,000 homecare workers, disabled and elderly consumers, and community members. As part of that campaign, homecare worker Pauline Beck, who had spent a day with presidential hopeful Barack Obama in 2008, penned a poignant letter to President Obama, urging him to intervene.

In June, disability advocates and SEIU homecare workers successfully filed an injunction against the state of California, halting the cuts to the state's more than 400,000 homecare workers. The Obama Administration supported the unions legal argument. The lawsuit stated that the wage cut violated the federal Medicaid law, the Americans with Disabilities Act, and the Rehabilitation Act.

Homecare Victory

"I was and still am convinced that the women of the world, united without any regard for national or racial dimensions, can become the most powerful force for international peace and brotherhood."

— Coretta Scott King, *I Dream a World: Portraits of Black Women Who Changed America*

The homecare workers' struggles and victories—past, present, and future—are well represented in scholarly articles such as the following by Linda Delp and Katie Quan of the UCLA Labor Center. These publications raise awareness throughout America that the labor movement is still marching forward and that women workers are at the forefront. The historical struggles and victories of homecare workers have served as a great inspiration to many other service workers who are also in the struggle to unionize. In this section, the authors analyze the unique challenges and opportunities that homecare workers faced as they built their union. They also explore the impact of homecare organizing on the Service Employees International Union nationwide and the ongoing debate of how America will care for its aging society.

The Homecare Victory
Organizing Workers in Los Angeles

Linda Delp and Katie Quan

When 74,000 homecare workers in Los Angeles voted in 1999 to join the Service Employees International Union (SEIU), it was the biggest organizing victory in the United States since 1941. These workers were finally "invisible no more." Action had turned their rallying cry into reality. How did they accomplish this remarkable feat? This section summarizes the challenges and describes the strategies used by SEIU Local 434B and the many activists who participated in the campaign.

The organizers faced a number of challenges. First, the workforce was fragmented. Workers were dispersed throughout the community and had no occasion to come together as a group. They spoke many languages—more than 100 in Los Angeles County alone. And low pay, lack of benefits, and sometimes the death of a consumer resulted in a high turnover rate: two of every five workers left homecare work within a year (Doty et al. 1999).

Second, there was no single employer with whom to bargain for higher wages, benefits, or better working conditions. In-Home Supportive Services (IHSS) issued the paychecks, but it did not have the authority to bargain with the union. Consumers hired and fired the workers, but they did not pay them, and consumers certainly had no ability to increase wages or expand benefits, as traditional employers do.

Third, consumers and the public did not necessarily support the organization of homecare workers. If workers formed a union, they might demand higher wages or go on strike against elderly and disabled consumers.

To deal with these challenges, the SEIU adopted three strategies: (1) organize and mobilize around day-to-day worker issues; (2) change policies to restructure the IHSS system to benefit workers and deliver better care to consumers; and (3) build coalitions between workers, consumers, and advocates.

Grassroots Organizing

When the SEIU began its campaign, grassroots organizing was the foundation. Without the interest of the workers, the union could not represent them. The high turnover rate necessitated constant organizing and reorganizing just to maintain support among a core group of 10,000 to 15,000 homecare workers statewide (Wilensky 2000).

Organization efforts in Los Angeles were particularly intense because of the

SEIU 434B members volunteer during James Hahn's campaign for Los Angeles mayor in 2001. This was the first time homecare workers organized to support a mayoral candidate. From left: Maria Cibrian, Blanca Carillas, Beatrice Hernandez, and Alfredo Martinez.

sheer number of workers. The SEIU's initial challenge was to find each of these 74,000 people. Los Angeles homecare worker Verdia Daniels, president of SEIU Local 434B and one of the original activists, described the outreach process: "We went to senior citizens' centers, doctor's offices, markets, churches; we even dug in trash cans to find lists of workers" (2000). Although reaching workers was difficult, convincing them to join the union was not. "It was phenomenal," commented Claudia Johnson (2000), former vice president of the L.A. local. "Once they saw a flyer or heard about the union, they would call in to the union for more information. . . . We were only getting $3.72 an hour at that time." Remarkably, the local was able to sign up 12,000 workers in a three-month period at the end of 1987. The union's message, which offered hope for improved conditions, had obviously resonated with them.

In the late 1980s, the SEIU established a satellite office, giving workers a space in which to come together. It also provided limited assistance for finding jobs, a precursor to a computerized registry system that was created in the mid-1990s.

While it recruited members at the local level, the union launched a statewide political action campaign that channeled the workers' grassroots activism into mass demonstrations and political action aimed at state policymakers. The SEIU participated in the campaign to raise California's minimum wage from $3.75 to $4.25, fought cuts in funding for homecare services, and filed a successful lawsuit over late paychecks, which prevented the state from withholding pay when the budget process was deadlocked (Chang 2000, 141). SEIU leader Ophelia McFadden (2000) credits these early successes for "grounding the operation and galvanizing the membership. People started realizing what could be done collectively."[1]

As the campaign progressed throughout the 1990s, union chapters held as many as fifty meetings each month throughout Los Angeles County to spread the union's political education message. Members used the meetings to plan legislative visits, write letters, and develop other methods to increase the union's political strength. Local 434B leader David Rolf (2001) stated, "Key

Among the workers from various unions at the 2005 rally is Luz Castañeda (wearing an emergency vest). A member organizer, she provided security for the 7,000 people who participated.

SEIU 6434 members at rally, 2007.

to the activism was a political focus. We organized to raise the minimum wage again in 1996 from $4.25 to $5.75, gathering more signatures to put the initiative on the ballot than any other union."[2]

Political successes were partly due to a change in strategy that allowed the union to mobilize more effectively. Organizer Rickman Jackson (2000) recalled:

> We started out organizing by zip codes, but then switched to precincts in 1996. We developed precinct leaders to walk door to door. We also separated members by assembly and senate districts and met with the legislators, telling them how

A northern county homecare union member holds signs supporting long-term care, Sacramento, 2009.

many workers were in their district and putting homecare issues in their face.[3]

The new strategy worked: legislators began to listen to homecare workers. Local 434B's executive board members described the union's growing political clout with pride, as Verdia Daniels (2000), noted:

> At first, we would go to the polls and vote; now we send questionnaires to the political candidates, then have town meetings with them. We tell them there's a crisis with homecare workers and consumers; we never leave out the consumers. Before, they closed the door after they got elected. We went to Sacramento and they would look at us—"what is this woman coming to my office for?" Now we push the door open if we need to. We worked very hard and walked very hard to get into those doors. Today they're coming to us, and we're holding them accountable.

Policy Changes

Early on, it was evident that policy changes were occurring in the homecare industry and that the challenge for the union would be to enter the policy debate with a plan that would strengthen the ability of workers to organize. Government agencies were experimenting with changes in services and funding in an industry that had become visible only in the 1970s. Consumer groups were already organizing nationally and statewide to influence policy making for various forms of homecare. One of these debates concerned the transfer of federal funds from nursing homes to independent providers.[4]

One of the first policy issues SEIU faced was to create an employer of record with whom they could bargain. The union's first strategy was to sue Los Angeles County for failure to bargain, thinking that the judge would rule that either the county government or some other entity must bargain with the union. To the union's surprise, the judge did neither, and the union was forced to find another method of establishing an employer of record.

SEIU then allied with consumer groups to create a Public Authority as the employer of record. In

A homecare worker speaks at a rally in Maywood.

1991, in the face of opposition from the governor and many legislators, the union proposed a budget trailer that would allow counties to establish Public Authorities as employers of record for homecare workers. During the same period, union staff worked with consumer groups, IHSS staff, and Assemblywoman Gwen Moore to sponsor legislation to obtain an additional $800 million in federal funds for the program under Medicaid's "personal care option." Accompanying this legislation was funding to establish Public Authorities in key counties.

After the Public Authority legislation was enacted, the union, in coalition with consumer groups, turned its efforts to Los Angeles County. The County Board of Supervisors opposed the designation of a Public Authority. The supervisors equated the action with unionization, and they opposed demands for higher wages, some of which would come from county funds. The

board agreed only to allocate some start-up funds for an independent study of homecare services. The union-consumer coalition launched the study and issued a report of findings (Coalition for IHSS Reform 1996) that became the basis for a Public Authority ordinance despite the initial opposition of the supervisors, the Department of Public Social Services (DPSS), and the county's chief administrative officer.

Throughout this process, the union waged a massive campaign to pressure policy makers. Workers picketed the offices of the Board of Supervisors and the DPSS and filed mass applications for zookeeper jobs, asserting that workers who cared for animals were better paid than homecare workers who cared for human beings. Union and community groups flooded the Board of Supervisors with letters and met with board members, urging them to establish a Public Authority (Rolf 2001). Ultimately these activities led to a 1997 ordinance that established a Public Authority in Los Angeles County.

Thus, the efforts to pass statewide legislation that allowed Public Authorities and, then, to pass local ordinances that set up a county Public Authority paved the way for union recognition and union bargaining. These victories would not have been possible without the coalition between the union and consumer groups.

Coalition Building

Coalition building with consumers became the means to achieve SEIU's organizing goals for several reasons. First, the disabled and elderly coalitions were already actively organizing for independent living through organizations such as the Centers for Independent Living and the World Institute on Disability. It was their advocacy that had won the establishment of IHSS in the first place. Any plan to improve conditions for homecare workers could not ignore the presence and strength of their movement. Second, since the consumers were politically strong, their support was critical. Third, a partnership between workers and consumers had the potential to become the core of an alliance that would include religious groups, community-based organizations, and politicians. The strength of a broad coalition that would support consumers' as well as workers' rights was precisely the leverage that the union needed to press its demands.

The merits of working in coalition were hotly debated among all players. Although some involved with the disability community advocated the worker-consumer coalition, citing its potential to leverage more funds for the IHSS program (Toy 1996), others argued that increased wages for workers could come only at the expense of fewer hours of care (Russell 1996). In addition, some consumers believed that the union would try to take over the IHSS reform effort and limit their personal autonomy. They also feared that the union would strike, leaving them without care. Consumer activists who supported the organization of homecare workers faced considerable criticism, as Blane Beckwith (2001) of the Americans Disabled for Attendant Programs Today (ADAPT) recalled:

> Some disabled activists told us that we were selling them out, but they didn't understand that the union was willing to change some of their practices. Unfortunately, there is still some dissension about unions among consumer groups that continues to this day.

Some within the union also did not see the value of working in a coalition with consumers. "There was constant pressure to produce numbers of new members," recalled Steve Wilensky (2000), former coordinator of the union's California campaign, "and not much tolerance for the time and effort it took to build ties with the consumer communities." Jeanine Meyer-Rodriguez (2001), director of SEIU's state council, noted, "Some people have tunnel vision, and they don't understand the importance of building a movement."

These tensions continued even after the union was organized and collective bargaining was taking place. Despite these problems, most union and consumer organizers agreed that the coalition was critical if long-term care was to be improved for workers and consumers alike. The ultimate success of the coalitions was largely due to the leadership within the union and the consumers' movement. Janet Heinritz-Canterbury (2001), an activist from the seniors' movement who worked with the union to develop a coalition at the state and county level, observed:

> Traditionally, unions used coalitions for media or public relations goals and not for internal strategic or tactical decisions. And, to many consumers, the union was a potential interference in the relationship they had with their workers. But winning any improvements in IHSS demanded that consumers and unions work together to develop goals and strategies. And there wasn't a lot of time for this complicated and often dicey process. Ultimately what it took was for these groups to develop a level of respect and trust that they were working for the same goals and an understanding that they needed each other in order to make improvements in their own situations.[5]

Conclusion

Each component of the SEIU's strategy— grassroots organizing, policy changes, coalition building—was distinct yet interrelated. Changing policy at the state and local level depended on a strong coalition of labor and community groups, which could not have been built without the organized voice of the workers. On the other hand, the workers could not have unionized without legislative changes and the support of the consumers. Finally, the strength of the coalition was based on the joint efforts of worker activists and consumers, as well as policies that guaranteed a role for consumers in Public Authorities.

Throughout California, similar campaigns over the past decade brought the total number of newly represented homecare workers to almost 200,000. The success of this landmark organizing campaign continues to be a tremendous achievement, inspiring workers with similar challenges, such as childcare workers, to begin organizing. The efforts of the workers, consumers, and staff organizers contributed new ideas and fresh inspiration to all those involved in rebuilding the economic and political clout of the labor movement.

Notes

This chapter was adapted from Delp and Quan 2002.

1. Ophelia McFadden was the general manager of SEIU Local 434-B during the period discussed.
2. David Rolf was the Local 434-B leader from 1996 through 1999.
3. Rickman Jackson was an organizer for SEIU Local 434-B during the period discussed.
4. See MiCASSA, the Medicaid Community Attendant Services and Supports Act, which was introduced as S. 1935 in November 1999 by Senators Tom Harkin and Arlen Specter; earlier versions were sponsored by other lawmakers.
5. Janet Heinritz-Canterbury was an SEIU coalition organizer during the period discussed.

Works Cited

Beckwith, Blane. 2001. Interview by Katie Quan, February 1, Berkeley, California.

Chang, Grace. 2000. *Disposable Domestics*

Immigrant Women Workers in the Global Economy. Cambridge, Mass.: South End Press.

Coalition for IHSS Reform. 1996. *Opportunity Now: Ensuring Reform to the In Home Supportive Services Program in Los Angeles County*. Sacramento: Keeslar & Associates.

Daniels, Verdia. 2000. Interview by Linda Delp May 6, Los Angeles, California.

Delp, Linda, and Katie Quan. 2002. "Homecare Worker Organizing in California: An Analysis of a Successful Strategy." *Labor Studies Journal 27*, no.19: 1–23.

Doty, Pamela, A. E. Benjamin, Ruth E. Matthias, and Todd M. Franke. 1999. *In-Home Supportive Services for the Elderly and Disabled: A Comparison of Client Directed and Professional Management Models of Service Delivery: Non-Technical Summary Report* Washington, D.C.: U.S. Department of Health and Human Services. Retrieved from http://aspe.hhs.gov/daltcp/reports/ihss.htm.

Heinritz-Canterbury, Janet. 2000. Interview by Linda Delp, January 30, Los Angeles, California.

Jackson, Rickman. 2000. Interview by Linda Delp, April 20, Los Angeles, California.

Johnson, Claudia. 2000. Interview by Linda Delp, May 6, Los Angeles, California.

McFadden, Ophelia. 2000. Interview by Linda Delp, May 25, Los Angeles, California.

Meyer-Rodriguez, Jeanine. 2001. Interview by Linda Delp and Katie Quan, May 30, Los Angeles, California.

Russell, Marta. 1996. "L.A. County Public Authority: A Zero-Sum Game." *New Mobility 7*, no. 38.

Rolf, David. 2001. Interview by Linda Delp, May 12, Los Angeles, California.

Toy, Alan. 1996. "A County Public Authority: An Empowering Solution." *New Mobility 7*, no. 38.

Wilensky, Steve. 2000. Interview by Katie Quan, December 28, Glencoe, California.

Ten Years Is the Starting Point

*"Change will not come if we wait for some other person or some other time.
We are the ones we've been waiting for. We are the change that we seek."*

— Barack Obama, after his defeat in the New Hampshire primary, 2008

The Los Angeles County homecare victory was a catalyst for workplace
and social change that positioned SEIU as a leader in the long-term care arena
with more than 580,000 long-term care members nationwide. Together these
women and men are building power and raising their voices in the workplace
and in politics. In this section, Gerry Hudson, who leads SEIU's work on
long-term care, reflects on the relevance of this historic victory.

Ten Years Is the Starting Point
Impact of Homecare Organizing

Gerry Hudson

Gerry Hudson, international executive vice president of the Service Employees International Union.

Being involved with the labor movement for several years has afforded me the opportunity to witness the incredible transformation that takes place when hardworking people say "enough is enough" and organize to ensure that they are represented in the workplace. Lives are literally changed. And while every organizing campaign is unique in its own way and a true victory, there are some campaigns that stand out—campaigns that speak to the strength of the human spirit and the commitment to go against all odds and to push through to success. The story of the courageous homecare workers of Los Angeles County—the women who strove tirelessly in the 1980s and 1990s to form a union—is to this day one of the greatest organizing stories ever. This campaign, which united more than 74,000 workers, is a testament to the power that can come from a few determined individuals.

I'm pleased this story is finally being told so that we will be better able to understand its impact on labor history, examine what we've learned from the journey, and apply these lessons as we prepare for the future.

It would have been enough if this campaign had been simply about 74,000 workers.

Even by today's jaded and cynical measure of what a "big deal" is, the ability to organize 74,000 workers is still staggering.

We hadn't seen a number like this attached to a union organizing campaign in over half a century.

In fact, you have to go back nearly seventy-five years, to the UAW's infamous campaign to organize the auto industry and its mass production counterparts in the areas of steel, rubber, and electrical work. That's the last time we saw such massive numbers—until 1999, that is, when the dream of a few African American women became a reality and SEIU Local 434B was established. Their success reignited the belief of what is possible even when workers are continually faced with public doubt.

It would have been powerful enough if this campaign had been only about women.

Even though women workers had high-profile and widely celebrated organizing campaigns, such as the SEIU 925 campaign in Boston and elsewhere, larger campaigns had been mostly dominated by men. And unlike the women who organized before them, those who led the Los Angeles County homecare campaign were low-wage workers in a nontraditional work environment, one that had no central location, no water cooler to gather around, and no common employer. Instead, these workers were

Yolanda Richards organizes pills for her consumer, 2007.

widely dispersed, providing in-home care to those in need.

What all these women held in common was the fact that the work they did was highly undervalued. These women moved forward—with many skeptics looking on and many challenges placed before them—and made what some referred to as the impossible, possible.

It would have been a historic moment and a signal of change to come even if this campaign had been only about who did the organizing.

Those behind this movement—Ophelia McFadden, Verdia Daniels, Gwen Green, and a handful of other determined women—were women of color working in a turbulent time for minorities in Los Angeles. Not since A. Phillip Randolph organized the Pullman porters back in 1925 had such a significant and successful organizing campaign led by people of color taken place. Although these two movements occurred seventy years apart, the workers shared an undying spirit to achieve what they were told would never be—a spirit and persistence found only among those who are always denied opportunity. For the porters it took twelve years to win their

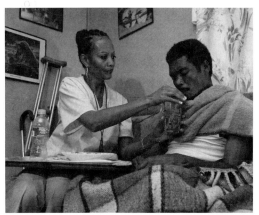
Pamela Hall feeds her consumer at his house, 2005.

first collective bargaining agreement with the Pullman Company. For the Los Angeles homecare workers it took nearly fifteen years.

To understand this, one only needs to look at the two streams of issues that crested and formed one river of opportunity: the difficulties that confronted low income organizing in Los Angeles County, and the sociopolitical reality that gripped black Los Angeles.

Graduates of the United Long-Term Care Workers' Union–Homecare Workers' Training Center in Los Angeles hold their certificates after completing homecare worker training, 2003.

In 1981, most of Los Angeles's garbage collectors—80 percent—were African American. Although the pay was relatively low, their salaries allowed them to have a middle-class lifestyle, benefiting not only their families but their communities as well. Nevertheless, the Los Angeles City Council considered privatizing those jobs, which would have reduced the hourly wage as a result. This threat was fought off, but others were around the corner, part of a new kind of inequality.

That inequality spread as immigrant populations in Los Angeles increased. But efforts to organize low-wage workers increased as well. From janitors to textile workers to hotel workers, immigrant populations (often pitted against workers of other backgrounds by employers) began to organize in a way folks had not seen before. This contributed to the shifting dynamics of work and started to alter the economy of Los Angeles. SEIU, seeing these changes and being part of them, knew that this was fertile ground and that something big could happen.

Empowered by the election of Tom Bradley as mayor of Los Angeles in 1973 and then disappointed by his dual losses in runs for governor in 1982 and 1986, the African American community in Los Angeles found itself in a quandary. Had it made progress? If so, by what definition? As Bradley stepped down in 1993, a sense of "unfinished business" was rechanneled, and along the way it took several strange turns. Just reflect on this list of incidents that preceded the apex of the Los Angeles County homecare campaign: the Rodney King beating, 1991; the trial of the officers who beat King and the subsequent unrest, 1992; Bradley steps down, 1993; O.J. Simpson arrested for murder, 1994; Simpson found not guilty, 1995; passage of Proposition 210, which raised the minimum wage, but also Proposition 209, which banned the state's use of affirmative action, 1996. For certain, the racial justice compass was spinning.

These events shook the labor movement out of some of its traditional notions, prompting organizers to develop new strategies. The leaders of the homecare campaign realized early on that to achieve their goal, new strategies had to be considered, strategies that reevaluated political power and made this organizing effort more than a "union battle."

Just like every organizing campaign before it, the homecare campaign worked to elect people to public office who were dedicated to lifting up working people. The campaign also discovered that there was much more to be gained through the political system than simply getting individuals elected. Instead of workers working for the political system, it was time that the political system worked for them. From this concept came the solution that made organizing 74,000 workers who held no common employer possible. By collaborating with legislators the campaign was able to pass legislation that created Public Authorities— the county-based employer of record for homecare workers. With the Public Authority in place, organizing and, later, negotiating were possible. This new strategy has become the cornerstone of homecare organizing throughout the United States.

Another new strategy that came from the homecare movement involved a new kind of partnership between stakeholders and community organizations. Unlike other campaigns, where community organizations showed their support based on economic impact or shared demographics, in this campaign those who were coming out to express their support were individuals who would also benefit from workers' gains. Some might have seen homecare consumers as a natural ally, but the reality was that these individuals ultimately had more to gain. A successful campaign would mean stability for the workforce that they depended on for daily care. By combining the voice of workers with the voice of consumers, a new voice developed, one that simply could not be ignored.

Now, ten years later, the union has larger numbers and more models.

Homecare workers rally in Los Angeles, 2008.

Workers took a page from the Los Angeles County homecare workers, and waves of homecare organizing campaigns washed across the country. As a result, 410,000 of the 1.2 million current homecare workers in the United States are now represented by SEIU—that's a density of 34 percent. From zero to 34 percent in less than ten years is a truly staggering achievement in the history of the American labor movement. It is a bright flashing signal of hope to workers and their families and communities.

Today's workers continue to take the movement to the next level while standing on the shoulders of their Los Angeles trailblazers. And as these workers continue to demand the respect they deserve and raise public awareness of the work they do, opportunities arise. One such opportunity gave our current president some first-hand knowledge about the challenges that homecare workers face. During the 2008 presidential campaign, the SEIU invited presidential candidates to "Walk a Day in My Shoes"—an opportunity for the candidates to learn about the lives of rank and file members. Senator Barack Obama took SEIU up on the offer and spent a day working beside Pauline Beck of Oakland, spending time with her family, assisting her with her care recipient, and gaining a true understanding of how difficult it is for homecare workers to make ends meet.

No one could know then what would become of candidate Obama, but it was already great progress to have the struggles of a homecare worker highlighted with such dynamism. Clearly, homecare workers were "invisible no more." They were live and in color. That day will always be a remarkable day for Pauline—and it had a real impact on President Obama, as he noted: "I don't mind feeling obligated toward homecare workers who clean bed pans every day for little more than minimum wage… I got into politics to fight for these folks."

And yet, it is not enough.

We celebrate, but we are equally engaged in what we must achieve in the next ten years. Homecare workers have made great advancements, but we must press on with the fight to stabilize what has been a volatile workforce by achieving the wages and benefits that truly reflect the work they do. As the population of our nation continues to age, the demand for care will only intensify.

According to the California Department of Aging, the number of residents sixty years of age and over will grow to 12.8 million by 2050—that's a 178 percent increase from 2000. Meanwhile, the number of Californians eighty years old and over will increase by 190 percent. With such percentages, the number of qualified recipients will also increase, and the homecare program will remain a target for budget cuts. The only way to ultimately protect the homecare program, and other similar programs, is to find a dedicated funding source that is secure and independent of the state's general fund.

As we look to the future, as we organize this sector and fight to protect the delivery of quality care, we must broaden our vision to embrace the entire spectrum of long-term care providers. Because of the victories and knowledge we have gained from the homecare campaign, we are better positioned to extend this success to the hard-working individuals who staff nursing homes, independent living centers, and assisted living centers, to private home care providers, and to workers in long-term care occupations that are just emerging.

By uniting all long-term care workers, we will not only build the capacity to vastly improve working conditions and standards for our members, we will also position ourselves and our coalition partners to be a leading force in seeking solutions for care accessibility for those in need. We will make real on the promise held by those courageous women ten years ago—the promise to protect the services that care recipients rely on and to be their voice in the fight to ensure their needs are a priority among Sacramento legislators.

Change Agents
Homecare Sheroes and Heroes

"A person noted for feats of courage or nobility of purpose, especially one who has risked or sacrificed his or her life for a just cause."

— *American Heritage Dictionary*

The homecare workers' victory would not have been possible without the outstanding work and commitment of its great leaders. Devoting countless hours to improving working conditions and the quality of care for the elderly and disabled, these leaders, activists, and staff members brought homecare out of the shadows and made homecare workers "invisible no more." The following oral history section provides the personal accounts of more than a dozen Los Angeles homecare campaign warriors who, in their own way, contributed to the 1999 victory.

Ophelia McFadden

Ophelia McFadden at a hearing for stakeholders in the 1990s.

Ophelia McFadden is a long-time community and labor rights leader. She joined the labor movement in 1968 as a staff representative for SEIU Local 434, the third largest county workers' union in the country, and ten years later was promoted to general manager. In 1989 she became the general manager of SEIU Homecare Workers' Union Local 434B. She retired from the labor movement in 1999.

I was not a stranger to the union movement. My daddy was a preacher and one of seventeen kids in his family. He was the pastor of First Baptist Church in Conroy, Texas. My daddy was also a union man who had the support of his church when it came to his other religion: union organizing. He worked in the oil refining business, and he died early. We had a nice living, me and my six brothers and sisters, so he enjoyed his life. He would always talk to us about what people should do in order to enhance their living conditions. He was heavily involved in the union in Texas. He made sure we understood that working with the union would bring about positive change. He told us to find jobs that had unions because they represented and fought on behalf of the people. I always enjoyed those stories, and it stuck with me.

> "The heart of the union is organizing, and it was my job to get out there and support somebody else who needed the help of a union. I recognized that need to organize homecare workers, and I did just that."

When I came to California, I wanted to know about the union life. I started volunteering at different unions in Los Angeles. This was in the late 1960s. I was involved with the community. I was an activist on racial issues and police abuse issues back then. My girlfriend had started working as an organizer with SEIU 347. Apparently it got so good to her, she wanted me to come down and check it out. I got involved in the union because I enjoy a good fight. I really do. Once I got involved with the union in Los Angeles, I fell in love. It was heaven to me.

I was the general manager of 434B, and I had my own union that had been organized and represented county workers. The heart of the union is organizing, and it was my job to get out there and support somebody else who needed the help of a union. I recognized that need to organize homecare workers, and I did just that. I knew I was going to organize them. People got to understand; you have to go to whatever extent you have to, to get some of the things you want in life, out of the union and out of your community. I knew early on that nothing was going to stop me or these workers.

First of all, there are so many ill people with so little dollars. I remember how difficult it was to see homecare workers take care of the disabled and elderly when sometimes the workers were about the same age as the clients. It's sad. That's why I became involved in homecare. It was a sad and difficult situation that these workers were in and still are in. Homecare workers

Ophelia McFadden (third from left) with Jesse Jackson (second from left), September 1983, Washington, D.C.

needed somebody to protect them. A lot of them were not educated. They needed somebody to go with them to show them some respect and hold their hands for awhile, until eventually they could stand on their own. They wanted the help. We just had to bring it to them. They were mostly women, working too hard for too little money. Through organizing, at least they ended up with some dignity and some job quality. And we are still working on that.

It wasn't easy organizing homecare workers. The hardest thing was to get them all together and get them signed up as members. This was no factory or plant floor where you could walk in and reach the workers all together. They were working in individual homes, working two and three jobs. But I remember the first meeting. We took a bus and drove through Los

Angeles picking up the workers. It took about two or three trips. We'd pick them up and take them back to the meeting. After awhile, the hall was crowded with people. House by house—that's how we organized.

We had events, barbecues, house meetings, whatever we had to do to get people together. And they would come, too. I sat down and talked to them, and if they didn't know what unions were about, I would explain that. And then I'd explain what would happen if you didn't have a union or if you didn't have enough members in the union: then it would be a flop. I stressed that we had to work as family. And that no matter the situation or the opposition, I would go down there and work

Ophelia McFadden at the Local 434B Convention for Homecare Workers, November 1991, Los Angeles.

you couldn't just be in the union and not be involved. As a member, I told them, you are going to be a leader, and you're going to be involved. You can't come out here and

"Homecare workers needed somebody to protect them."

as a family, and they would do the same. And they all did.

For some reason they trusted me, probably because as the person representing the union, I didn't go down there to the L.A. Board of Supervisors with the idea of being a partner. I was not a partner to management. They were the problem standing in the way of homecare workers in the end. When I would go to the Board of Supervisors, I'd go down there to raise holy hell and tell them the real deal. That's what you need to take on management, and the members trusted me to have those skills. And the members really did trust me. They saw that the union would go to the mat for them.

I knew up front that organizing homecare workers was going to be a fight, a showdown between L.A.'s poor and vulnerable and the wealthy establishment. I let the workers know this. I told them that

not get involved in a union that's working for you. And if they couldn't be active and involved, then you couldn't be in the union. You were snatched out of the union. That was my philosophy on member leadership in the union.

The community was essential to a victory. When I came into organizing the homecare workers, I knew all the people in the community. I knew all the weapons and the people I needed to touch. Remember, my father was a reverend, and so we started in the churches to organize homecare workers. At the time labor was so racist, so antifeminist. Labor was pretty bad for a long time. Labor was a bitch. Before homecare, I had spent much of my time in the community fighting for the rights of people who wanted to join the union and fighting for the rights of people inside the union as well. Because some of these unions are not right. I spent a lot of time educating the community about workers' rights and the need to bring affirmative action into the union. I brought a lot of community into the union movement in Los Angeles. These community and political leaders and organizations began to see that people needed to eat and that fighting for the survival of working people was important. The homecare worker would start off with nothing—no employer, no steady paychecks or hours, and no job protections—even though the money for homecare work comes from the public tax dollars and should be spent responsibly on the best care possible and best working conditions possible.

Ophelia McFadden at a hearing for stakeholders in the 1990s.

Union members must know that we owe something to humanity. When we do a job, we must do it well. We owe something to humanity, and that was the whole issue with the Public Authority and establishing an employer for the workers. That was a major fight. The county or the state is paying you money or a salary through the public tax dollars; therefore, the public must ensure there is a level of humanity for the people who are receiving services and for the people providing that service.

I used to give the Los Angeles Board of Supervisors hell when we went down there. We would have rallies down there during the meetings, and I would tell them, "Supervisors, these are human beings just like you think you are." Supervisor Pete Schabarum would get so mad, he looked like he wanted to hit me with a chair. But that's what we had to do to get the board to act like human beings. We had to stay on them and stay on them and rally and call them out and tell the truth about how homecare workers were being treated. I enjoyed my job, especially fighting with the Board of Supervisors. When we went down there, we were fighting for the people, and homecare workers responded by packing the chambers. We started going to the meetings with a small group. Before you know it, we had masses, thousands of workers standing with you. What else could the Board of Supervisors do? They had to respond. That was the breaking point; then the workers voted to join SEIU.

This campaign is important to remember. It shows the value of the union and the power of people coming together. Labor is on the downhill now. You don't hear about it in the mainstream as much, in the home, in the neighborhoods, or in the churches. You just don't hear people talking about the importance of fighting for good jobs. The union needs to get back on track. It bothers me to see the disconnect between the union and the community. We have people who can barely make ends meet. Yet they've been told to talk against unions and to stop unions.

Part of the problem is that people are coming here from different parts of the world taking over jobs that we worked hard to get a union for. And these people, for no fault of their own, are taking these jobs and are working for whatever they can get. I do understand it, and I'm not angry with them. The point is, everyone has got to eat. Employers and American policies are every day shipping more people over here from other countries. But people in America want to eat and have a place to live also.

The point is, right or wrong or indifferent, all of us must eat and unless we come together through the union movement, we face unimaginable poverty and suffering in this country. The homecare campaign was a very happy time in my life. I've been involved in the labor movement for twenty-eight years. I've really enjoyed every minute of it. I retired some years ago, but I'm still in the loop. People still call and ask me questions to get my opinion on things, and I love it. People can say a lot of things about me, but they have to say that I worked. These workers were black people like me, and I wasn't going to stand there and let the people be disrespected.

Verdia Daniels

Verdia Daniels speaks at the convention to authorize the homecare workers' union, 1999.

Verdia Daniels has been part of the homecare workers' struggle for almost three decades. She has served as a member organizer and as the first president of the local. She continues to work with the union as President emeritus.

My name is Verdia Daniels, and my first homecare job was in 1975. Before that I was a member of the Bakers and Confectionery Workers Union in Los Angeles. I came to homecare when my husband had taken ill. I had a little girl, and I wanted to have flexible hours. I decided to take on a patient that was in my church. She had asked me to go with her to visit a nursing home, my first time ever in a nursing home. At the nursing home I saw what was taking place, how there were too many patients and not enough people there to take care of them. It was understaffed. That's what I could see as the reason why they couldn't take care of the patients. I was asked by some of them to take them home. There were many of them that were walking around, and my understanding was, why are they here? How come they

> "In the beginning, I remember, I was off of my job at 3:00 p.m. and would go to the union office, and sometimes I didn't leave until 1:00 a.m. We had to do it all. We had nothing to work with."

Verdia Daniels participates in a demonstration for homecare workers, about 1999, Los Angeles.

meeting that there were other homecare providers other than myself at the time. I realized there must be a lot of them around. I think on that particular flyer about the union, it said there were 42,000, and that was unbelievable to me. I wanted to be in on it to see what I could do to help. I knew about unions, and I knew that the homecare workers needed it to get some benefits.

They talked about the organizing of homecare workers in Boston, and Ophelia McFadden had been in Boston and was part of the organizing. When she returned home, she started talking to her neighbor who did homecare and found out they were making barely minimum wage and no benefits. Ophelia decided then and there she wanted

can't be in their own homes? But I'm a single individual, and I don't know anything to do to help them.

So I began taking care of the woman in my church. So when this opportunity came,

> "We started meeting, and the interest of the homecare providers grew. We let them know that we as homecare providers needed to make a change, and this is going to make a difference in your lifestyle, in your family."

which was in '87, to join the union, I jumped on the bandwagon, because this is my time, I thought. I can do something, whatever it is I can do. So that's when I wanted to start up organizing and recruited other homecare workers. I received a notice in the mail, "Let's organize homecare workers in L.A." And there was a little card on that little flyer to mail in if you were interested, and I mailed it in at the post office before I left. Within a few days, I had a call: Would I be able to attend a meeting? I decided to attend because of the low, low wages, no benefits whatsoever, and the pay, which was only $3.72 an hour.

That was the first meeting, and it began with seven members. The organizer talked about training for the homecare providers, and I was interested. I learned at the

to organize homecare workers in Los Angeles County. She discussed it with Kirk Adams,[1] and they decided to go to President Sweeney.[2] He said there was no way that there was going to be any organizing of homecare workers in L.A. County, but she insisted, "One day, I am going to organize homecare workers." And knowing her, she hounded him to death until he decided that, "Okay, you can start." That's what happened. That's where we began organizing at that point. We had very few organizers, and we had to use the few people that we were able to recruit.

Naturally, the Los Angeles County Board of Supervisors would not work with us. We had to go from door to door, knocking on doors, trying to find out if there were homecare workers. We went to doctor's

Verdia Daniels with Local 434B members, Los Angeles, about 2000.

many hours and what time the volunteers could come in. And we didn't have very much money to work with; therefore, we'd be hungry sometimes, so that's why we would always say we had pizza and Pepsi every day. I don't like pizza today; I don't drink a Pepsi.

It was a dedicated group of people. We became one big family. So this was how we got started. We started organizing members from different areas because we knew we didn't work on the same worksite; therefore, we had to start opening offices in different areas; there was about sixteen area offices in L.A. County that were opened up immediately. We started growing. We started meeting, and the interest of the homecare providers grew. We let them know that we as homecare providers needed to make a change, and this is going to make a difference in your lifestyle, in your family. We had a lot of single parents that were trying to raise their children that did not want to be on welfare. They wanted to work, and they had three and four jobs, because they didn't have enough hours—because the $3.72 an hour, that was very little to try to raise two or three children on.

We started growing and growing and growing, and before we knew it, in the end of '87, I think, we had our first convention. And we turned in 12,000 cards to the Board of Supervisors that we had collected that wanted to become union members. Of course the board refused to see us, but we managed

offices, to the grocery stores, even riding the public transportation, watching people. We wore white painter's caps and jackets saying "homecare workers," and had people asking us questions, "Oh, what do you mean by homecare workers?" You had your form to give them and explain. That's how we first started recruiting.

When we started the campaign, we only had about six organizers. And there was the director and, of course, the general manager, who was the founder, Ophelia McFadden. We worked out of an office of SEIU Local 434. Kirk Adams was the campaign director, and Ophelia McFadden was the general manager. It was a small group of us, but the list of volunteers grew to countless people and hours as the campaign took off. In the beginning, I remember, I was off of my job at 3:00 p.m. and would go to the union office, and sometimes I didn't leave until 1:00 a.m. We had to do it all. We had nothing to work with. All of our mailing had to be done by hand. We made phone calls up until 9:00 p.m. After that we would stay and stuff the envelopes to the ones that we had called. Then we kept a chart on the wall of how to have the sheriff escort us in, and we were able to drop off the cards. I still have a copy of one of those little cards and an article from our first rally, which was published in the *Los Angeles Herald Examiner.*

The rally was at a county facility. We had about 150 people; we were carrying our banner. No one from the county came out to talk with us, but we were out there yelling and telling them our issues: livable wages and benefits and training.

One of our first things was to try to increase the pay, and we did get that increased to $4.25 an hour. As a matter of fact, I remember we were in downtown Los Angeles, and we were rallying there. We were told that we didn't deserve $4.25 an hour because homecare workers only dust and sweep the floors and make the bed. And that's what they thought. They didn't know that we were doing more important things sometimes than a nurse was doing. Maybe they would give you forty hours, and you were doing sixty hours a month for that consumer, because that's what they needed, and you just couldn't walk away from them.

Notes

1. Kirk Adams is currently the executive director of SEIU Healthcare Division and he oversees all of the SEIU National Healthcare organizing projects.
2. John Sweeney is president of the AFL-CIO.

Lillibeth Navarro

Lillibeth Navarro advocates for homecare workers' rights, 1997, Los Angeles.

Lillibeth Navarro is a disability activist who spearheaded efforts to organize the disability community as part of the homecare workers' union campaign. She currently serves on the board of the Personal Assistance Services Council (PASC), the Public Authority for IHSS in Los Angeles County.

I formally met the disability movement in 1985 when I was working at USC [University of Southern California] part-time. I was a full time student. There was a big protest. It was the national protest of ADAPT. I almost didn't want to go. That weekend I saw for the first time about 200 people in wheelchairs, empowered, protesting. I went, "Oh, my God." So that was my initial baptism to the disability rights movement officially. It changed everything for me.

From the time I decided to become an activist, when I met the movement, our homecare workers were down in the trenches with us. They were there, getting us up in the morning, helping us prepare. They were partners from the start.

When I started working for an independent living center, I was a benefits advocate there, but I was still in training. There were advocacy meetings around IHSS, and I wanted so much to be a part of that. But because I was still in training, my supervisor said, "No, your focus is this." So I could not participate. Eventually I left my work, and I was free to explore this thing. Here we were being organized and coming to meetings sponsored by SEIU. There were a couple of us, old friends from the L.A.

disability community. That's where I began to really see what the issues were.

Right from the start, when I went to these meetings there was very strong opposition in those meetings. The union was being accused as this big organization with all the funding, with all the people power, and the legislative heavyweights on their side. And here we were, this puny little movement. I really had to think very seriously about the issue. It confronted me in the most basic way. It came down to: I'm a disability rights activist. I am fighting for my rights. These are workers. They're fighting for their rights. Should there be a contest of rights? So what I finally came up with in

I was immediately beset with accusations of being a union stooge. So to answer that, we formed IRAPS—IHSS Recipients and Providers Sharing. At first, it was RAPS—Recipients and Providers Sharing. Since we were being accused of being union stooges we immediately wanted to proclaim, "No, we're not!" We were very determined to prove our colleagues wrong about us. That's when we really consolidated IRAPS. We were going to be the consumer organization that mobilizes the consumers. We were not going to get union funding alone. We were given a start-up grant of $5,000. We used that just to get the basic things that we needed, then we decided to find our own

"From the time I decided to become an activist, when I met the movement, our homecare workers were down in the trenches with us. They were there, getting us up in the morning, helping us prepare. They were partners from the start."

my thinking, praying about it actually, was moral consistency about people's rights. People, disabled or not disabled, are people. They have the same rights. So the clarion call I thought to propose was a consistent, ethical social justice.

So at that time we were forming a study group of seniors, disabled-rights leaders, and union members that came together and really studied the issues with an open mind. I was elected to head the group. The study group was formed to figure out how to organize. It became the strategy group. It's a study group in the sense that the union helped us with the research. We brought in our own of what we knew about the system from the disability perspective. The seniors brought their own perspective from their own experiences. So it was a challenge, but at the same time I became a lightening rod for the disability community.

fiscal sponsor, because we did have our own 501-C3. We applied with SSG [Special Services for Groups], at that time a forty-year-old organization that was hatching programs like an incubation organization for future nonprofits. SSG sponsored us for a good eight years. IRAPS and the coalition became the big project of our lives. Everything was secondary for all of us. We knew on a personal level what it meant; all of us were dependent on it. The workers and consumers, too, were living the inadequacy of the system.

The Los Angeles County Board was really our main focus. The Department of Public Social Services did a study that concluded that the Public Authority model was not going to be good for L.A. County. Can you imagine? I mean the Board of Supervisors was resistant to the idea, because they feared that they were going to be asked to

Lillibeth Navarro, disability rights activist and the executive director and founder of Calif-Communities Actively Living Independent and Free, 2000.

as the best model of care for people, because homecare is family friendly, it's very respectful of people's choice. It's also cost-effective, caring for people at home where you don't have to uproot them from their families, you don't have to deprive them of all rights. You don't have to trap people in nursing homes.

So the IHSS coalition has taken a totally different direction. The coalition is now the Long-Term Care Project. I think the coalition should focus on getting the money down here to California and down to L.A., but also making sure that not only the workers get the funding, the Public Authorities get the funding. I like the fact that we have a registry now, a countywide worker registry where people are screened and trained, that there's real consumer

spend more money. Apart from the DPSS study, the state gave L.A. the money to study the IHSS. To do our own study, we went to

"It came down to: I'm a disability rights activist. I am fighting for my rights. These are workers. They're fighting for their rights."

visit the seniors. We would do a two-hour presentation. Every IRAPS presentation had us, the consumers, talking about the Public Authority. Some people from the union were talking about the Public Authority from the workers' perspective, and we had a raffle. So the consumers, this is what we were doing. Of course the union had their meetings; they had their chapter meetings. And then of course the seniors had also theirs.

Our persistence led to our victory and the establishment of the Public Authority. It was a very persuasive argument for homecare

voice. We have a lot to do in that area, too, because L.A.'s so big and the Public Authority board is so small. I think for now, since the Public Authority is new, they can concentrate on growing the consumer base, but my challenge to the Public Authority is that it keep challenging itself to bigger and better things. They can do focus groups. They don't have to do the advocacy because their hands are tied because they are a quasi-government entity, but they can be an organizing force that empowers the consumer community to then be the change advocates. They should work with independent living centers like us towards that goal. I think for now the Public Authority, it's new, but my challenge to the Public Authority personally is that it challenge itself, because the Public Authority is happy with the registry and that's fine. But we cannot stop there. We cannot stop there.

Lillibeth Navarro participates in a demonstration in Los Angeles, 1997.

Addie Parsons

Addie Parsons, executive board member of ULTCW, 2007.

Addie Parsons, who was one of the early leaders in the drive to organize homecare workers, is currently an executive board member of ULTCW.

I received a card through the mail, and it said, "Join the union." The job I was working on before, when I took the job, the man told me, he says, "Save your money, because before I would have a union in here, I would close it down." So when I got the card through the mail, I was all excited, "Well, I'm going to be a union member," not knowing that I had to come in, work, and do all this other stuff. So I signed the card and I sent it in.

Then there was a lady, she constantly called me to attend the meeting, and I would say no. Then finally she broke me down, and I attended the first meeting, but I thought when I went in, this was going to be a big thing. I go there all dressed and everything, and I listened, and the things I heard Verdia Daniels and Carter say, how they were trying to get people to help, and it just went to my heart. I started going, and it was just like an attachment that I couldn't break myself away from. I would listen to Miss Ophelia McFadden speak, and she was such a strong person. And I said, "This is what I need."

"The money I earned, in turn, I had to spend it on her because her income was limited and the medications were four hundred dollars a month, which I had to take care of."

She was just so strong with what she said. She was the person that I admired, and I just started attending.

I started homecare work maybe in '85. My mother, she was ill, and being the only child, there was no one else to help her but me. By that time I had created a job for myself. I was a dressmaker by choice, and I had to shut that down to take care of her,

Addie Parsons with Assemblyman Merv Dymally, about 2000.

because she was in a wheelchair for fifteen years. Actually that was my only client, my mother. I took care of her until she passed. I had a lot of free time, because on the little money I was getting, I had to have three other people to help me with her, with the lifting and everything. The money I earned, in turn, I had to spend it on her because her income was limited and the medications were four hundred dollars a month, which I had

was my first rally that I had gone to, the year that Pete Wilson announced his candidacy for governor, . . . and I gave the speech outside on the megaphone that I was crashing the party.

It was just like something that was attached to you. You wanted to do it, and, mind you, there were only seven women that were doing this, and we were family, and we were close. There were no divisions

"There were no divisions in what we were doing. It was just like a family."

to take care of. So I had time on my hands where I could attend meetings. Whenever there was a meeting, I was there.

I remember one lobby we did in Century City, those people were so dressed up. We were out up on this ramp yelling, waving flags, and we had one girl to go in, and they denied her entrance. She went in, and then everybody wanted to know, "What are they doing?" Then one man came and said, "Why are you here?" And we told him, and he said, "Oh yes, you need better pay" when we told him the amount of money we was getting. That

in what we were doing. It was just like a family. You know the good thing about it, when I go to these conventions, and they say 434B, everybody recognized 434B. And then they would ask me, "Will you tell me how you guys got started?" Naturally I gave them the local number and the president's name, and they went from there, because I'm very careful about giving out information. But I feel good when they say 434B, because I know the struggle I've been through to help 434B to be where it is today.

Lettie Haynes

Lettie Haynes, founding member of the homecare union.

Lettie Haynes has been a homecare worker since the early 1980s. She has helped organize new members into the union and is currently on the executive board.

I've always been into unions. I worked in an accounting place way back in 1965, and I was in a union then, so I know union work. Also my father was in the carpenter's union. So all my growing up was involved with him and the union. He would have people coming through our house. Then you would have people who were running for different offices, and they would come in and talk to you. You would gather your family and the neighbors. He would come in and talk to us about the union; then we would go out and do volunteer work for

> "We weren't getting enough money, and we weren't being recognized. It wasn't being recognized as a job. I felt that it was a job, and we needed to get the right pay for it."

him, pass out flyers, whatever we could do for him.

I was working on this job, it was a government job, and they discontinued the funds, so I got on unemployment. A friend of mine told me about homecare work, and I said, "I have unemployment, but I've got a lot of bills." I had a new car, and I had a house note to pay, and I said, "Oh, I don't know how I'm going to make it." So she told me about this man that needed a homecare worker. I'd never done homecare work before, but when she explained it to me,

I said, "Oh yes, I can do that." I met him, and that's how I started into homecare work. I did it for a couple of years, and I started at $4.25 an hour. I was making $4.25 and it was 1980. When it got to 1987, I was still at that $4.25 an hour, and I'm saying to myself, God, when are they going to do something about this, because everybody's getting raises, and the homecare workers are falling behind. So when they started sending out

Beatriz Hernandez (left), Anita Allen, Lettie Haynes, and Verdia Daniels at union headquarters in Los Angeles, 2000.

the things about a union, I think I heard about it happening in New York first. On the East Coast they had the homecare workers union. I said, "Oh, they're never going to have it on this coast, because it's going to be too hard to form." Then, when they started telling me that they had, I said, "I don't believe this. I've got to see."

I was looking at my paper one day, and I saw Verdia Daniels. I knew her from

Being a homecare worker and talking with homecare workers, I knew the inside problems of it, their plight, how we weren't getting justice and dignity for the work we did. We weren't getting enough money, and we weren't being recognized. It wasn't being recognized as a job. I felt that it was a job, and we needed to get the right pay for it.

A lot of times we would donate our own time because we weren't getting paid if we

"We, as homecare workers, didn't have a way to come together. That's what the union helped us do—come together. It showed us how to come together."

years before then, and I said, "Oh, this is Verdia, one of my old-time friends." I got the number and I called her. She said, "Oh yes, I'm starting another chapter in South Central. Come down and help me." I said, "Oh yeah," because I wasn't doing anything but homecare work then. I was working like three days a week, so I said, "Oh yes, I'll come down and help." I went down and started helping her taking the minutes and stuff like that for the meeting. From there I moved to the executive board, and I've been there ever since.

didn't have enough hours. With my client, I did that. A lot of times I had to work over, because he only had fifty hours when he first started. It ran over that because he was a senior, and he had brittle bones. If you made a wrong step, he might break his leg or ankle. When I started working for him, it made my hours a lot longer, because I didn't want to leave him there by himself. That was my burning inspiration—to get homecare workers up and organized.

In 1997 we developed a new chapter, and that's been going ever since. As an area trustee, I would come to meetings, find out what the homecare workers were doing. They were complaining about the hours, and, of course, the wages were down. I said, "Wait a minute. You've got to come out to your chapter meeting, and that way you could find out about everything that's going on in the union, and that would keep you up on the information. That way, you wouldn't have to ask." A lot of workers didn't understand about the union. A lot of them hadn't been in unions before. So they were hesitant at some times. Some of them knew a union would make us better.

We, as homecare workers, didn't have a way to come together. That's what the union helped us do—come together. It showed us how to come together. In our divisional meetings, we'd come together and talk about different things going on with us everyday with our clients, how we could make our job better and make it better for our clients. After they came and found out that the union was really helping instead of hurting, then they started coming in, talking about it, and getting information. As we went on, as we organized, they said, "Well, everything is better now from what it used to be." Before, some of them would get cut off of their checks or wouldn't get their checks on time. With the union, we kept working until we got those checks, and people started getting their checks on time, and they had some recourse. When they found out they did have rights, it was better.

We still have a lot of challenges. I feel we will defeat those, like we've been doing. Together we can make it. If we stick together we can do it. When my grandchildren are off from school, and we have to go down to the Board of Supervisors, I take them with me. I give them a banner and tell them to hold it up and go march, so they see it firsthand. Sometimes when we're out doing volunteer work, passing out literature, going door to door, I take them along with me. I let them see how it's done. They get a big kick out of it. I tell them it's important because by us doing this, it makes it better for them. It makes it better for the workforce. I even go back to civil rights, how what Martin Luther King did made it better for them and how what we're doing is going to make it better for the homecare workers to come. I explain to them that it's important to give back to something that is meaningful.

Gwen Green

Gwen Green in 1999. She was the community relations director for the organizing campaign from 1989 through 1999.

Gwen Green is a retired civil rights and community activist. She led the effort to build community support for the homecare worker organizing campaign, organizing the collection of hundreds of petition signatures and acts of support from local churches, community organizations, and elected officials.

My grandfather was a Pullman porter.[1] Then he became a Pullman porters' instructor, but he also worked with A. Philip Randolph, and he was one of the organizers of the Pullman porter benefit association. So my father worked at the Pullman Company, worked in their shops, and he was the chairman of their union. They didn't have social workers or nothing like that, so my grandfather was kind of like a social worker. He really took care of the problems of the Pullman porters. In fact, if a Pullman porter got in any trouble, they'd come to Mr. Williams,

my grandfather. If they'd been jailed or something like that, he would always get them out. Then later he decided that the Pullman porters needed training, so he came up with the idea of having a trainer for the Pullman porters. So it was his idea, and he became the first Pullman-porter trainer, and he went all over the country training the Pullman porters.

I got married, and I went to live in Boulder, Colorado. There, my husband and I organized the NAACP [National Association for the Advancement of Colored People] in Boulder, Colorado, which was back in 1944.

In Boulder they would not let the black people go to the restaurants or anything. I also was a member of the Western Christian Leadership Conference.[2] We started having rallies, and then we had major fund-raisers. We raised thousands for Dr. King, and so I became acquainted with Dr. King.

In '65 they were going to have this voter education program. Andy Young, Ambassador Young,[3] came out and asked me, would I come down south and be the assistant to Hosea Williams.[4] So I went down south and spent the summer, and the project was called SCOPE, Summer Community Organization and Political Education. They recruited students from all the major universities all over the country. In the first week of June, about 3,500 students from these colleges came in to Atlanta, but they had to agree that if they became a part of the project, they had to live in the black community, live in the black peoples' homes, and eat their food. They couldn't come with a lot of money. They had to work for the black people; the black people didn't have to work for them, basically. So we were in six states and one hundred and twenty counties, so that was successful.

Then I was also involved in politics. I was one of the founders of the New Frontier Democratic Club in 1960.[5] At that time we were trying to elect a candidate. Forty-five years later, it's still the largest Democratic club this side of the Mississippi.

In the '60s, '70s, and '80s, I worked on the campaigns of most of the black elected officials. I worked for Tom Bradley as his office manager a few times.[6] And then in the

Gwen Green and Lori Dunn at a rally to certify Local 434B, 1999.

NAACP, I was secretary of the branch. But then they hired me to be the branch secretary, and that's when I met Ophelia McFadden. She was a volunteer. About '63, her and Audrey Edwards, they both volunteered, and then they became organizers for the union.[7] And I guess Ophelia worked her way up and became the head of 434.

Some of the ladies, homecare workers, came and asked her to help them with organizing. So she called me and said, "Girl, I need your help." Ophelia and I were partners when we worked at NAACP. She said, "You're the only one I knew who'd be willing to come to work." I met her—how many years ago—twenty-seven years ago. She was a baby. But Ophelia just worked hard, hard, hard, and fought like a dog for the homecare workers. Because she was busy, I would be the one to go out in the field. I know I came there to work, but I really didn't know what I was coming to do or anything. She said, "I just need you." I started working with her, helping. My job was to get to the ministers and to all the organizations in the various cities to get them to sign the cards, and we used to have them sign saying that they recognized and they felt that homecare workers should be recognized and have their wages.

Remember, I knew Dr. King before the March on Washington.[8] I met Dr. King in the spring of 1959, and I started working for him at what was the Western Christian Leadership Conference in 1960. I knew all of the ministers from my work with Dr. King and the Civil Rights Movement. We had to educate the ministers. The church members have homecare workers, and some of the ministers' mothers have homecare workers. It was about people. I remember one time, I was talking to some of the ministers, and one said, "Let me tell you, I don't know what I would have done if I hadn't had a homecare worker for my wife." It wasn't hard to sell because it's about their mothers or their sisters or their members. So what's right is right, and we had them. In fact, in all the political campaigns, every time I'd go on a campaign, the first thing they'd do is say, "What did you do with the ministers?"

Mobilizing the clergy is very, very, very difficult. There's a new breed of ministers now, so I have not worked with them. We used to go down to the board and protest and whenever we protested, I always had ministers. So it was getting pretty hot and heavy. One time Yvonne Burke said she didn't care how many ministers Gwen Greene brought down there, they weren't going to give us a raise.[9] She was quite adamant about not getting a raise, but we prevailed. One minister had a little church, and he was president at one of the Baptist ministries, and one day we had a march, and he had some alligator shoes. He got to walking, poor baby. He said his feet

were throbbing so bad. But he got through it, he participated, and it wasn't hard.

I remember the day when they finished counting the cards determining whether the members wanted to become a union, and that was a great victory. Ophelia was sick then, and she wasn't too active. I remember Andy Stern came. He wanted just to get her there. So she came out, and I remember Zev Yaroslavsky, and he got up, and he said how Ophelia trained him.[10] Ophelia trained a lot of the white boys that were halfway decent.

The community, they were supportive, but most of our activity was with the members. The members were the ones that cared and had the enthusiasm, that were willing to go to jail and sleep on the floor and everything. It was the members. We had some organizations sometimes that would come out at nighttime when we had demonstrations, but it was the members that really did this. They fought hard and long.

I really enjoyed the campaign. Most of the time, it was fun and exciting. And when the people would go down and talk, they'd work hard. One time we had a demonstration and went down to the Hall of Administration, and they had a bus, one of those buses that have the elevator for the handicapped people. That was thrilling times. I had goose pimples because they had about a hundred wheel chairs, and it was always exciting to me. I was ready for whatever they were going to do.

Really, I guess homecare work is one of my loves, and then working for Dr. King in my experience down south. The homecare workers' fight was a crusade just like Dr. King. It's about raising people into dignity and getting their rights. They were just the biggest things. My political stuff, that was alright, and we had victories. But we helped masses of people, and my main interest in life is trying to help people. So being a part of working with Dr. King and then coming and being a part of the homecare workers and seeing how far they've come, words can't describe it.

We're training the homecare workers, so the people that are ill are getting better care. The

Gwen Green and Rickman Jackson at a community hearing, about 2003.

homecare workers, they're getting more money, they're being trained. We have all kinds of training programs. If they want to be a homecare worker, they can be, but if they want to go all the way up to being a nurse, they can. We've got that available. We have dental programs. We're starting a credit union. It's very basic, and it's filling the need for thousands and thousands of people.

That is what a movement is about—real change. I remember some years ago, many of the field workers that worked with us, they called me up and said, "Mama, we miss Dr. King. Where is Dr. King?" And I said. "Well he ain't coming back. Just go on and make a movement." But you have to work. They got to the place where all they wanted was to jump up, call the press, and have a press conference. "Bottom up," I said. "No, you go on and do something, and you start out with two or three people, and you start doing something. Pretty soon you don't have to call the press up. They'll come. You can get a movement." I said, "Honey, there is so much to be done, especially nowadays, because we're going back by leaps and bounds. So you just go find yourself something."

I gained a lot from the homecare campaign

because I felt like I was doing something. I don't like sitting around doing nothing because it's not worth something. I can see that I was a part of a great movement, and I can see that I did a lot to make this world a better place. I've been blessed to have that opportunity. Because I worked with Dr. King, one of the world's leaders, and I can say truly, that he, his wife, and children, were my friends. And homecare workers, that union is going down in history, so I can say I had a part in it. It's a good feeling. A lot of people don't have it. You ask them, "What have you done in your life?" Nothing. I have grandchildren, and I hope they'll have children, and so I've tried to make it a better place for them. Someone helped me, and so I just carried it on.

Notes

1. African Americans frequently worked as porters on Pullman trains. Phillip Randolph helped organize these workers into the Brotherhood of Sleeping Car Porters union in 1925. The BSCP became the first African American labor union to sign a collective bargaining agreement with a U.S. corporation. See http://www.apliliprandolphmuseum.com

/evo_history4.html.

2. Western Christian Leadership Conference is an organization that is committed to continuing the nonviolent opposition against social and economic injustices that was initiated by Dr. Martin Luther King Jr. King founded the Southern Christian Leadership Conference in Atlanta, Georgia. See http://www.georgiaencyclopedia.org.

3. Andrew Young was a top aide to Dr. Martin Luther King Jr. during the Civil Rights Movement. He also served as vice president of the Southern Christian Leadership Conference. See http://www.cau.edu/p_releases/BioAmbassadorAndrewYoung.htm.

4. Hosea Williams was an aide to Martin Luther King Jr. and became a principal leader of the Civil Rights Movement. See http://www.georgiaencyclopedia.org/nge/Article.jsp?id=h-1009.

5. The New Frontier Democratic Club was founded in 1960 by African American leaders in Los Angeles. It is the largest and oldest Democratic Club in California See http://www.newfrontierdemocraticclub.org/.

6. Tom Bradley served on the Los Angeles City Council from 1963 to 1973 and was elected mayor in 1973. See http://www.biography.com/search/article.do?id=9223579.

7. Audrey Edwards was a friend of Ophelia McFadden; she introduced Ophelia to organizing at SEIU.

8. The 1963 March on Washington was led by civil rights leaders and included more than 200,000 demonstrators who demanded jobs and freedom for African Americans. During this event, Martin Luther King Jr. delivered his "I Have a Dream" speech. See http://www.stanford.edu/group/King/about_king/encyclopedia/march_washington.html.

9. Yvonne Burke is serving her fourth term on the Los Angeles County Board of Supervisors. See http://burke.lacounty.gov/.

10. Zev Yaroslavsky is a member of the Los Angeles County Board of Supervisors. See http://zev.lacounty.gov/scripts/zevbiohtm.

Loretta Stevens

Loretta Stevens, director of the California Homecare Council, in 2007.

Loretta Stevens was an SEIU senior organizer and a member-organizer specialist in 1990 when she joined the homecare organizing campaign. Stevens trained members on how to organize the union from beginning to end. She has worked with many SEIU local unions in the western region and has served in a variety of roles. Today, as the director of the California Homecare Council of SEIU and UDW/AFSCME (United Domestic Workers/American Federation of State, County and Municipal Employees), she coordinates homecare work throughout the state of California.

I come from a community organizing background. I grew up in Berkeley, so there was a lot of activism in that city—the Black Panthers, antiwar movements—so I was always involved in struggles.[1] I did organizing against police brutality and around health access issues and as president of the Signal Hill Tenants Association when we fought against an effort to displace and remove African Americans from that community. My husband was a member of the union over the years, and he was actually working for SEIU before I started to work for SEIU. He encouraged me to get involved in worker rights directly through the union. My first campaign was with SEIU Local 99,

> "My experience then and now is that homecare workers are some of the most generous, loving, and giving types of individuals, to be able to do the work that they do and for the little they earn."

Loretta Stevens speaks at a rally to protest proposed wage cuts for homecare workers, June 2009.

older African American women who were making minimum wage and were clearly underpaid for the work they did. I always felt it was like a bunch of mothers being abused for their kindness. My experience then and now is that homecare workers are some of the most generous, loving, and giving types of individuals, to be able to do the work that they do and for the little they earn. I identified with them and the injustice towards them. I often thought that if homecare workers were men, they would not be making minimum wage and with little to no benefits. I think because women were the predominant gender of the workforce, they were being exploited.

My early observation of the campaign was also that it was very intense. Leaders of the campaign worked long hours. They worked hard because there were a lot of workers. Every block, there was probably a homecare worker. It was like

the classified school employees union. I was on a team of nine organizers that recruited about 2,000 new members in about three months. My work on the campaign allowed me to do a year-long internship program with SEIU. That gave me a theoretical foundation of unions, and I got to talk to a lot of leaders in the labor movement and got a lot of training over the years.

"They understood it was an investment in themselves. So you would get homecare workers, the poorest of the poor, to join, because they knew that their sisters and the union were about the opportunity for voice and real positive changes."

Some time later, I worked for the International, and we shared offices with SEIU Local 434 general manager, Ophelia McFadden. So I was always around homecare, even though I wasn't directly working on the campaign at that time. This was around early 1990. At the time, I worked with a lot of locals statewide on different projects. I did education and training, I did organizing, I did bargaining, I did whatever—strike support, whatever.

I was surrounded by homecare workers. I was impressed by the work, the energy, and the spirit. They were mainly

an underground economy, and invisible. The union campaign brought in visibility: "Invisible no more" in the struggle for dignity and respect.

There were a lot of workers, and organizing them was a challenge. The campaign operated mostly door-to-door. Catching them at home was like a needle in the haystack. I remember helping out with outreach for the campaign, signing people up and doing house visits. They were so poor. Their housing and living conditions weren't stable. You know, we didn't use the phone very much. We went door to

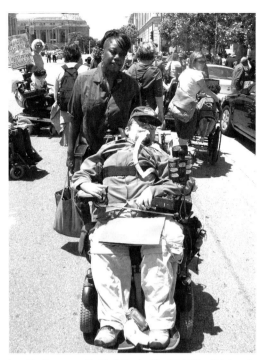
Loretta Stevens with Mark Beckwith, ADAPT activist and disabilities advocate, 2009.

qualities. They are active, passionate, and have a persevering spirit. This propelled the homecare organizing in the '80s and '90s and is still there in the union today.

Two years after the Los Angeles victory, I became more involved with homecare. In 1999, United Domestic Workers/AFSCME and SEIU reached a partnership agreement. Statewide there are fifty-eight counties with homecare workers represented. SEIU was organizing in some and AFSCME in some. So when I came aboard, it was to help to expand and coordinate organizing statewide in California. The California Homecare Council was established as the entity representing all homecare workers in the state. I became the council staff responsible for coordination between UDW/AFSCME and SEIU.

My role involved working with the staff of the different unions in different counties, trying to come up with creative approaches for field and solidarity work between the two unions, which had had a history of rivalry around jurisdiction and a lot of antagonism that I hadn't been a part of in the past. I knew the agreement was in place. Everyone involved realized it was in the best interests of the workers. We understood we would be stronger with the two unions working together and the two staffs looking at ways to do team approaches in the unorganized counties.

When lobbying at the capitol today, homecare workers turn out by the hundreds regularly, while other unions have maybe fewer workers. It's important that the workers know what the union's doing and be a part of it. Workers leave at one or two a.m. in the morning to get to Sacramento by bus. Many of them are seniors and have some physical challenges, but they come and participate.

door. We reached out to the workers in the communities that they lived in, a lot of project areas, a lot of poor areas of the community. It was always amazing to actually reach a worker. I always like house visits, because you get to hear directly from the workers. And a lot of homecare workers wanted to join the union. Homecare workers would get it. But the optimism and hope was there with the commitment. When we were signing workers up and they were still unorganized, many voluntarily contributed ten dollars a month towards the organizing. There was no union, but these mature women understood it takes money. They understood it was an investment in themselves. So you would get homecare workers, the poorest of the poor, to join, because they knew that their sisters and the union were about the opportunity for voice and real positive changes. And homecare workers have some unique

We have a homecare coalition that consists of all the stakeholders: the unions, consumer activists, the Public Authorities, advocacy groups for the disabled and the elderly. It shows the strength of the union, of the coalition, and it has paid off. You see it in the numbers.

That's why legislators know homecare in the capitol. And there is bipartisan support for the issue, especially because of the cost savings compared to institutionalization. Even talking to different Boards of Supervisors today, like in San Bernardino, every family is touched by the need of elder care, a parent, or even a personal disability. It just crosses all ethnicities, classes, genders. So even a person like the governor's wife, Maria Shriver, acknowledges that father who has Alzheimer's and needs homecare services. So people know the direct value of that type of service and support. The people deserve it. Quality of life issues are involved, and you live longer when able to remain in familiar surroundings while receiving care. The homecare workers and the coalition educated the public on this issue through media, community outreach, and people's direct experiences. The public supports and understands now that people have the right to stay in their homes—it saves the state money over all—and that homecare workers are critical to maintaining that reality. The L.A. campaign sparked a lot of national organizing by SEIU around homecare. We've organized in Michigan—about 35,000 workers there. I worked on a campaign in Wisconsin where we organized homecare workers from an agency. In Washington and Oregon we now represent homecare. What happened in L.A. and what's happening in California now is a model for how you raise industry standards among a shut-out group of workers that didn't have an employer and build lasting societal values around what homecare means to the most vulnerable— frail elders and persons with disabilities.

Note

1. The Black Panther Party was a political organization founded in Berkeley in 1966 to promote black self-reliance. See http://www.blackpanther.org/legacynew.htm.

Amanda Figueroa

Amanda Figueroa, secretary-treasurer for SEIU Healthcare ULTCW, Super Division 2, in 2007.

Amanda Figueroa had been a homecare worker for more than thirteen years when she got involved with the union in 1998. She was part of the first member-organizing program. She currently serves as secretary-treasurer of SEIU Local 6434, where she leads all immigration-related campaigns and the nursing home division.

I worked in Bolivia, as a teacher. I worked two years in the province, in the fields, because that was a requirement. You have to do some social service work. After that I came to the United States.

I came to this country because of, first and foremost, the economy. A teacher would eventually get the equivalent to fifty dollars a month or less. I am the oldest of the four of my siblings; in total, we were seven. My father had passed away, and I had to care for my younger siblings, but I didn't make enough money to support them.

I came to America all alone. I arrived in Los Angeles—well, first to Mexico with a Mexican visa. They told me that, in order to get off the plane, I needed to pay two hundred dollars for the passport. They let me get off the plane and said, "We will not charge you anything until you get to Tijuana, and from there, someone will take you." When I arrived in Tijuana, they told me, "You have to pay one hundred and fifty dollars if you want to get out of the airport." I had to pay that money. They had already given me an address where I could go and where the people would cross me. So I crossed by running through the hills with a person. I arrived with a family who let me stay in their home until I found a job. I found a job and met one of the family's cousins. We both left and rented an apartment, and I have been here ever since.

One comes to think, you come to this country, and the only thing you want to do is work. But you don't think about your rights being violated or if you are risking your life in the workplace or if, come tomorrow, you will be seriously injured. You don't think about it. The only thing you want is to earn money—or as we say in Latin-America, "dollars"—in order to send them to your country, because those "dollars" will multiply over there. Who cares if something happens? All you think about is earning money.

I came here alone, with nothing, with no one. I didn't have any family members

Amanda Figueroa (left), Olga De Leon, and Zoila Ramirez protest budget cuts at the rally in front of the Ronald Reagan State Building in February 2009, Sacramento.

Mexicans, the farthest they will send you back will be to Tijuana." So I learned the Mexican national anthem, Mexican history, the words, and the slang. I was lucky to have a close friend, who I consider like a sister, teach me. I lived amongst Mexican people in order to survive, in order to stay in the United States the amount of time I had planned.

"One comes to think, you come to this country, and the only thing you want to do is work. But you don't think about your rights being violated or if you are risking your life in the workplace or if, come tomorrow, you will be seriously injured."

here. In Latin American countries, they don't explain that we need a social security number to work, or some sort of identification, or a green card. When I got here, I spoke Spanish, but it seemed as if I didn't because the way of speaking was different from the Mexicans. During that time, I had to learn the history of Mexico, because they would tell me, "If INS gets you, they will send you all the way back to your country. But if the INS gets you, and if you know the Mexican history and speak like

I never considered or took into account that I would meet my husband. I didn't plan on staying here. I planned on returning to Bolivia, but things didn't happen like that. I was only going to stay in the U.S. for three years, because my dream was to go back to Bolivia and continue teaching. I came to the U.S. in the late 1970s. I began working in a sewing factory, later in a store in the meat department, and then I began working by caring for a lady named Esther.

Amanda with a client at an SEIU Super Division 2 meeting in 2007.

far as wages go—$3.25. I had asked the social worker, "Sixteen hours per week?" And she answered, "No, Amanda, sixteen hours per month, which means you have to work eight hours every two weeks. That's four hours a week." "But I will not be able to survive on that," I replied. She said, "That is all we have to offer for now. You either take it or leave it. It's your decision. It's up to you." So I had to take it. The lady I worked for made me work every day but only for one hour. I would commute from my house every day, which would usually take about thirty minutes each way, plus the cost of gas. When I would get there, the lady would ask me to start right away, and I would end up working up to two hours. This means I would never get paid for that hour. What I mean is that I would work two hours but only get paid for one. That was the first experience I had working.

I began working as a homecare worker in 1981. A friend of mine talked to me about it and asked if I could help her take care of someone, and I agreed. At the time, my daughter was very young, and this was something I could do for my family. I didn't know about unions or that I was part of one. I just didn't know. I thought I was alone. Perhaps I thought this way because of the type of building I worked in or because the person I cared for lived alone or because I wouldn't see anyone else come and go. I thought I was the only one. I thought that if there were other workers, they would probably come in but work different hours. I would tell myself, I am alone. I don't work with anyone. My husband would ask, "Who do you work with? Who are your coworkers?" I would respond, "I don't work with anyone else. I think I am the only one that does this job, because I don't see anyone else."

I began working with a woman who gave me only sixteen hours per month, and I was getting paid $3.75 or $3.25 per hour. In 1985 that is where we were at, as During Christmas time, other workers began asking me who I worked for, and we would compare stories and notes. Around those days, I greeted an African American lady by wishing her a merry Christmas. She replied by saying, "We will have to work that day." I replied, "Why would we have to work if it's Christmas? Isn't it a paid day off for everyone?" "No," she answered, "you will have to come to work. Only those who are part of the union get the day off." "Union? I don't belong to a union, because I don't even know if one exists for this type of work. Where is that? Where are they?" I replied.

She would care for another lady in the same building. They were all senior citizens and every time we would wash their clothes, we would get together and chat in the laundry room, despite the fact that the ladies would prohibit us from talking to one another. They would say that talking with each other wasn't right, that it was simply gossip. "You will become a gossiper" was the first thing they would tell us. "You will go to the laundry room to wash clothes when I tell you. If you find someone there, you will not talk to them. That is what I order. You talk to someone, you no longer work for me." So we would always have to obey them. If we didn't, they would say, "I don't want you anymore. Leave." So that is the point; the worker always feels scared, thinking to herself, what am I going to do? For years it was like this, until 1998.

[Hugo] Camacho came to my house and by this time, I had already worked for many people, and I had worked in another building where there were many other homecare workers. When he got to my house, he addressed me as Amanda. I denied that that was my name. "I am not Amanda," I told him. I did this because in 1986, there was an amnesty, so people were saying that this was a way to catch undocumented workers and that they were going to send us back to our countries. So as an immigrant who is fearful, you protect yourself and you say, "No, that is not me." When I told him that wasn't me, my five-year-old daughter heard and told me, "No, mommy, you are Amanda." I just stood there embarrassed, but I didn't know who this person was or what he wanted, so I lied once again and denied my real name. He asked me if I was a homecare worker. I asked him, "Who told you this? Who gave you my address?" He replied by saying, "I come from the union. You have a union." When he said "union," I knew what he was talking about because of my father, he belonged to a union which in my country they call it *sindicato*. I looked at him with doubt and asked, "Are you speaking the truth, or are you trying to deceive me?" He repeated, "You have a union." I look at Hugo and asked, "Okay. What is your name?" He replied, "Hugo Camacho. My name is Hugo Camacho, and I am an organizer for SEIU, your union, and I have come to talk to you." I let him in and said, "Come, here is my husband."

In 1987 my husband began working for Tianguis Vons.[1] When he began working for Tianguis, organizers signed him into the union and . . . I would go with him to the meetings and be a part of the contract negotiations. During the contract negotiations, they would tell them, "Those that work in produce will receive such-and-such pay, and those that work in the meat department with receive such-and-such pay." I would tell my husband, "No no no. Don't accept that. Why would they pay those that work in the meat department more then those that work in produce, if both workers are part of the union?" I was always involved in my husband's contract negotiations with [United Food and Commercial Workers] Local 770.

My husband sometimes felt uncomfortable because I was a woman and was involved with his union. In our culture, how could a woman be involved? He would say, "You know what? Stop getting involved in that." I would respond, "No? Why not? It's about your benefits, our family's benefits." That's why, when Hugo came to my house,

I immediately invited him in and asked that he also let my husband know what he had to say. That is part of the culture of a Latina woman. We involve "the head of the household" in any decisions we make, even if we have a clear idea of what we are going to do.

Hugo described what I did at my job. He knew what he was talking about. It's not as simple as coming in and saying, "I am organizing a union," if you don't know what the job entails. He later asked, "Do you want to be involved in the union?" I enthusiastically replied, "Yes, of course." I worked in a building where only ladies

"Our struggle, our fight wasn't simply economical. It was a struggle to waken the workers' consciousness. It was to defeat fear, so they would not be scared to claim their rights."

that didn't know anything about the union worked. Hugo told me, "We are in the process of organizing ourselves." I asked him, "Have you really organized the homecare workers?" He replied, "Look, we have tried, but we don't know the workers. You guys don't work at the same location. There are 74,000 homecare workers, Amanda, in Los Angeles County alone. That is why during these past thirteen years, it has been really difficult to organize, because nobody knows each other." In 1986 I found out through Helen that there was a union, or that one was starting up. It was easy to talk to her, because we worked in the same building, and she lived in South Central Los Angeles. After I stopped working there, I lost contact with her and didn't hear anything about it since then. I told Hugo, "Give me your card. I remember the blue cards. Give me some of your cards."

I began talking about the union in the building where I worked, and I began organizing them. I stressed how important it was to for us to form a union, to join the union, because that meant we were claiming our rights as workers. There were African Americans, Anglo Saxons, there were Latinas, there were Asians. I explained to them that we didn't even have a doctor and asked them if they knew we had a right to receive medical attention. I also stressed how we were getting paid such low wages for the jobs we did, especially because we always ended up working extra hours. I also shared what I had gone through and the experiences I had lived, like having been fired from a job for not having worked on New Year's and how we were never entitled to any vacation time.

I would mainly organize in the laundry rooms. Soon enough the word got around, and the older women who had homecare workers started disliking me because I was causing the workers to be discontent with their working conditions. The women would make the homecare workers work more hours than they were paid for in order to keep their job. After awhile the woman I worked for would tell me, "Go ahead. Continue doing what you are doing. I support you. Just don't involve me in anything you are doing because then later, they will not want me here. Tell them that I am also scolding you, that I don't agree with what you have to say. But you continue, continue, continue! They have already told me that you are putting ideas into the worker's heads, that you are leading them in the wrong direction. But you need to find a way to convince them to join the union and that they don't have to tell those they are working for."

We came to an agreement. We agreed that joining the union would not only benefit us but also benefit them. We would be able to work more hours for them because many of them needed more hours, but they weren't given to them. So they would reply, "And who guarantees us that?" I would reply, "If you and I fight together, we will accomplish that the program be changed, because that is what this is—a program." And they would say, "No, you have too many dreams. That doesn't work. We are older than you, and we know better." I would answer back, "Exactly. With your wisdom, you need to support us, because we are all in the same situation. We all get paid too little. We have a lot of

Amanda speaks at a "get out and vote" rally in Los Angeles, 2004.

work to do within a small amount of time, so we always have to be running around. On the other hand, if we unite and have them change the program, we could work more hours for you and be able to accomplish more."

I could say most of them accepted the idea, but they had to think about it a lot. A lot of them opposed. I can't sit here and say they all agreed, but most did. They would accept, but they wouldn't get involved because they said the matter was political, and they couldn't get into political things. They could only get involved in matters that had to do with recreation, etc., etc.

Our struggle, our fight wasn't simply economical. It was a struggle to waken the

workers' consciousness. It was to defeat fear, so they would not be scared to claim their rights. It was a cultural thing. One of the women, Mrs. Eligia, would say with that same fear I once had, "Yes, I am Mrs. Eligia." I would tell her, "I am Amanda. I am a homecare worker just like you." Then she would say, "No no, I am not Mrs. Eligia." I would answer, "I once did the same thing!" She replied, "No, really, the only person I take care of is my son." So I replied, "Well actually, you are a homecare worker, and I take care of other people, so both you and I are homecare workers. I want to talk to you." She answered, "Look, come on in and talk with my husband. Whatever he decides, I will do." So I had to go into her home and speak with her husband. I told him, "I am a homecare worker, and I am organizing my coworkers to form a union and have elections. We need this right away, because we don't have such and such. . . ." He replied, "You know what, Amanda? It's a pleasure to meet you. This country was formed and prospered because of labor unions. I support you." He told his wife, "Mi hija, sign because this is good for your future, our future, and our children's future." Our struggles and obstacles made us strong, our strength gave us power, our power gave us a voice, and we became invisible no more.

Note

1. Vons Tianguis-format stores, now closed, had bilingual employees and signage and featured traditional Latin American produce and other foods imported from Mexico. *Tianguis* is a Mexican word used to describe an open public market.

Janet Heinritz-Canterbury

Janet Heinritz-Canterbury.

From 1992 to 1999, Janet Heinritz-Canterbury organized and coordinated statewide and county efforts to promote the establishment of the Public Authority. She serves on the governing board of the Personal Assistance Services Council (PASC), which is the Public Authority for IHSS in Los Angeles County, and the board of Direct Care Alliance, a national coalition of long-term care consumers, direct-care workers, and healthcare providers who pursue public policy and health care industry reforms.

T raditionally unions used coalitions for media or public relations goals and not for internal strategic or tactical decisions. But winning any improvements in IHSS demanded that consumers and unions work together to develop goals and strategies. And there wasn't a lot of time for this complicated and often dicey process. Ultimately, what it took was for these groups to develop a level of respect, trust that they were working for the same goals, and an understanding that they needed each other in order to make improvements in their own situation.

Collaborating to Improve
In-Home Supportive Services:

Stakeholder Perspectives on
Implementing California's
Public Authorities
By Janet Heinritz-Canterbury

PHI

Cutting edge report issued in 2002 that analyzes the role of California Public Authorities, IHSS, and homecare stake-holders and provides model for counties seeking to establish Public Authorities to ensure quality care and quality jobs in the homecare industry.

Lucinda Ray

Lucinda Ray, ULTCW executive board member, about 2008.

Lucinda Ray joined the homecare workers' union in 1992. She has brought new members into the union and served on the executive board as secretary and area trustee. She continues to organize workers as a staff member of SEIU Local 6434.

I got a letter inviting me out to a meeting. I thought, yes, I'm going to go, because most of my family's jobs have been union. My dad was a railway worker, and I belonged to Canon Electric, which was represented by the autoworkers' union. I worked for Solar Lighting, which was Electrical Workers IBEW. I've been union all my life. I was raised a union child, and I was told, "You've got to work union if you want decent wages and benefits."

I never knew that homecare workers had a union. I got my homecare workers union card in 1991, and I'd been doing homecare since 1978. I left my job—a very good job, a top -paying job—to care for my Dad. He lost his leg, and I just didn't want anybody to take care of him. And I had promised my parents I'd always take care of them. I started taking care of daddy and went down to $3.72 an hour. My husband and I discussed it, and we were doing okay.

So in 1991 we went to a union meeting in Bellflower. The organizer would tell us all about the homecare workers and how they have struggled trying to get a union going.

And I said, "Yeah, great," so I just signed my card. I joined the union that night. I knew I had to be part of the struggle. Then I talked to people there and told them how important a union was for us. Some of them signed a card that night. The organizer said, "You're going to be a leader: you're going to be an activist."

Then they started holding monthly meetings in Bellflower. I went down there. Myself and one other lady came out. They used to bring two bags of groceries and raffle them to the people that were there—two bags of groceries and only two people, so I always got a bag of groceries. This happened a couple of times.

Then David Rolf called me on the telephone, and he said, "I've heard some good things about you. I'd like you to come to our E board meeting." I really just loved it from the beginning. When I got up and spoke, David went and made a surprised facial expression. Everybody sat back, because I have a very outgoing voice; then he talked to Verdia Daniels, and there was a seat on the executive board. About two meetings later, Verdia and David approached me and asked me if I'd like to be on the executive board, a trustee, and I went, "Sure." Now, I had my daughter. I was taking care of my dad, and I went to the meetings. But, it was worth it. It was a fight. It's a plight, and I know I wanted to help as much as I could. And I've been here ever since.

I think the thing that we did that was so important was to actually come in contact with people, explaining what the union can do and how important the union is. I don't just say, "We're having a union." You have to explain and actually talk to them. That's what we did. Myself and Rickman Jackson started looking for sites for our chapter meetings. We have this meeting in Long Beach, but that's not going to be good enough. We have to start getting chapters all around, because our homecare workers are so spread out. Rickman and I would go down and find a place and knock on doors. And we got Long Beach going, built up and running well. I kept telling Verdia, "We need a chapter in Norwalk, where I'm from, my area," I would say. "There's a lot of homecare workers in Norwalk." So then, she kept talking to David. Finally, we got the go-ahead. Esperanza Deanda and myself reserved the library in Norwalk for our first meeting. About sixty people came out. Norwalk was one of the biggest chapters. We would meet once a month at the same time; the third Wednesday of the month, at 6:30. So these people knew. We stressed, "Put it on your calendar. Come and learn about the union." And then new people would come in, and we'd sign them up right then and there. We'd tell them, "It's so important. If you want to get ahead, you have got to join this union." Now so many years later, I'm still an organizer. And I love my union and homecare workers.

"I joined the union that night. I knew I had to be part of the struggle."

Beatriz Hernandez

Beatriz Hernandez outside Local 6434, Los Angeles, 2009.

Beatriz Hernandez is a founding member of SEIU Local 434B. She has served on its executive board and has been a volunteer organizer. Still an active member of the union, Beatriz works at the SEIU 6434 front desk, and she continues to provide homecare services.

I came to the United States in 1980 from Chametla, Mexico, where I had been a secretary for a large fishing company for twenty years. After visiting the States on vacation, I knew that this is where I wanted to be. When I arrived in the States I did a number of various jobs to make ends meet for me and my three children. Times were tough. Minimum wage was only $3.25 an hour, and our small one-room apartment cost us $200.00 a month. I remember when I would go shopping to buy soup, rice, potatoes, and beans for my family, I would see people's shopping carts piled with food

and I thought: One day I want to be able to do that for my family.

I became involved in homecare as a care provider in 1989 after the garment factory I was working in closed. A very good friend of mine from my hometown in Mexico, Maria Rodriguez, worked at Angeles Plaza in downtown Los Angeles and told me about the opportunities that existed as a homecare provider to residents at Angeles Plaza. In my first day visiting, I had found four consumers who needed help with different chores. Since I really enjoyed working with older people, I knew this

Beatriz with a consumer, about 2009.

so many hours walking from house to house and telling workers about the union. I had the union in my heart! We were the pioneers that were going to make this happen. Forming this union was very important to us all.

When the day came and 434B became our official union, I felt very proud. We had worked so hard to make this dream come true. And with the new union came a lot of responsibilities for us all.

job was the perfect match.

A few years later, in 1992, homecare workers at Angeles Plaza were invited to come and learn about being a part of a new union. The union was looking for care providers to help organize workers. I signed a card that night and started helping out whenever I could. I never said no when the chance came to help out.

Our goal was to talk to as many home-care workers as possible. We volunteered

This union is my second family—my life. When I come to the union hall, I forget everything. I'm happy it's a part of my life. I've learned so much because of the union. I have gone to so many classes that have been offered. I've even learned to speak English during this time. The union has always been there for my family and me and has brought solutions when they were needed. This is the reason I give back . . . because the union was always there for me.

Cecilia Rivas

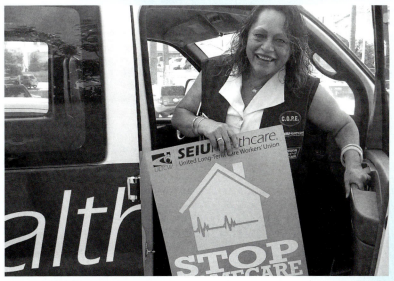

Cecilia Rivas at Local 6434 in 2009.

Cecilia Rivas has been a homecare worker for over twenty years. She started with the homecare movement in 1987 as a volunteer member organizer, knocking on doors and connecting with her fellow homecare workers. She played an integral role at each stage of the union's formation. She currently works as a greeter at the Los Angeles Union Hall.

I started in the very beginning of the homecare movement—in 1987—through the person I cared for at Angeles Plaza. He was the president of the Coalition for Senior Citizens and was also involved in many other organizations for seniors. Rudy Barragan was a staff member organizer who first came to Angeles Plaza and spoke with my client, then, as I mentioned, my client involved me.

So many years we sacrificed. At first, we were only four people in our small meetings, then we knocked on the doors of other workers, often running from dogs and having doors slammed in our face. That time we were working out of a small office building.

When we would go door-to-door to get more workers involved, I would tell them: "We are the same. I'm a homecare worker too, we do the same work. I'm talking to you member to member." And when we did that, they understood. We were talking from our hearts and how we thought about our jobs. Nobody knows how hard we worked in the beginning to organize workers.

It was a tough struggle for homecare workers because the Los Angeles County Board of Supervisors didn't recognize us. From the very beginning we fought many times with the supervisors for homecare worker rights. For me it was very exciting. When we got our first contract we were so happy; that's why we had our t-shirts that said "Invisible No More."

I knew I would like this union. Our leaders worked hard from their hearts, not from pay.

Cecilia Rivas at a homecare rally, about 2008.

Our wages started at $3.25—minimum wage. We fought to increase our wages; we went to markets to have people sign petitions. We were successful. They increased our wages. And we even went to the White House, and when President Clinton signed the legislation, I was there! For the first time, I went to Washington and saw the SEIU office.

Today, my roll in the union is to help people. I help at divisional meetings. If we are leaders, we have the responsibility to know everything and tell the members what we know. So they don't think we are hiding anything.

The labor movement is very proud of the homecare organizing victory because nobody knew who we were. They didn't believe that it would be possible to get so many people organized. Because we were such a small group at first, nobody believed we could win.

We have to sacrifice our family and sacrifice ourselves. I gave my own time, my own gas, my own lunch, etc. But I'm still saying, that's okay, that's fine, I'm still here! That's part of our lives.

I have learned a lot from the union. I didn't know I had so much to give, and I didn't know what to expect. I'm proud to be a union member. We had our goals, where we were going to go, and it feels good to achieve them. You have to give your heart, you cannot expect to get paid. If you believe in what you are doing, you feel good. That's how to build leaders. You're working hard and you don't expect anything back.

Rickman Jackson

Rickman Jackson.

Rickman Jackson was born in Jamaica and began working with the L.A. homecare campaign as a member of the organizing staff. He later became the organizing director and then the lead of Los Angeles County District 2, which mainly focused on South Los Angeles. He is currently president of SEIU Healthcare Michigan, which represents over 55,000 homecare workers, RNs, nursing home aides, and hospital support staff throughout the state.

I n Jamaica there were six of us. Primarily my dad survived on repairing shoes, and farming was on the side. He did a little bit of fishing and everything else he could to make ends meet. Even though we were poor, there was this dream that my life would be better than that of my parents'. That was a motivating factor I think. I left Jamaica for a number of reasons. One, I wanted to go to college, and my sister was already in the States. She is a registered nurse in Miami, so I came up to live with her. As a typical male, I wanted to see what life was all about, so I came to California to stay with friends. I got my regular allowance from her, and that's how I survived on my own before I found a job.

I was twenty-one years old when I first got involved with the social justice movement. I was in San Francisco and I was fascinated by this movement to turn the projects into privately owned housing. So I got involved in the organizing of the residents. This was just the residents wanting to own where they were living.

I guess it was my calling to do organizing.

Rickman Jackson addresses a homecare rally, about 2008.

targeted recipients lived mostly in South Central, and it so happened that I was working out of SEIU 660. As soon as the election was over, the project director recommended fifteen of us to work for SEIU. I got interviewed a day after the elections, and I went back to San Francisco. I was called a couple of days after the interview for a statewide homecare organizing position, working out of Local 616. I started working that same week, so this was about mid-November 1992. In January of the following year I was sent down to L.A. for training, and I ended up staying on with the homecare campaign. Ophelia said, "I think you should stay here." She moved me from

I mean, I knew what it was to grow up poor and it hit me right there and then— oh, this is not the poor that I'm used to. I saw people having to wait for a check to survive, which was much different from

> "I'd say, even as we speak, I'm still learning about homecare. It is a challenge every day. It does not matter how much time you spend or how much you think you know, it is a learning process. And every time you deal with it, you learn something. From the outset, we knew this wasn't just a job."

growing up where my dad had a farm where he could grow the crops and feed his family, so it was a different kind of poor. It was clear that when it comes to poverty here, you're in a box.

After the housing campaign, I got involved in a voter registration campaign, and a group of about twelve of us registered over 28,000 young voters in San Francisco, mainly in the projects. The project director chose four of us to come down to L.A. to do a GOTV project for Clinton/Gore. So I came to L.A. from San Francisco in September 1992, and we got to do this special project, which was an attempt to take adults off welfare. I think this was the first attempt to cut welfare recipients. The

the International payroll and put me in the local payroll so I could stay and organize in L.A. County only.

I guess none of us had an idea what we were getting into. I'd say, even as we speak, I'm still learning about homecare. It is a challenge every day. It does not matter how much time you spend or how much you think you know, it is a learning process. And every time you deal with it, you learn something. From the outset, we knew this wasn't just a job.

People would say, "I'm just doing this for a friend or for my family," and, "If I wasn't getting paid, I'd still be doing it." So it was hard organizing the first time around. Nobody wants to talk about it. Even if you're a homecare worker, you wouldn't talk about it. For example, if you are doing homecare, and I'm doing homecare, and we are neighbors, we would not talk about it because it's low-paid, minimum wage. You're not a nurse; you don't have to go to school to do it. It wasn't looked at as part of the workforce. You didn't want to say you were a homecare worker, especially if you were taking care of a family member. "You shouldn't get paid for to do this. Why are you getting paid for this?" people would say. So I think that's part of it; people didn't feel they could come together.

out there knocking on doors, is that when you are talking about training, wages, and benefits, you have to talk about quality care if you want to unionize the workforce. Just talk to them about quality care, whether it was relatives getting care for mothers, daughters, fathers, or a stranger. How do we provide quality care? How can we change this? Even today, wherever you go across the state and talk about quality care to the consumers, they will stop to listen.

To me, workers didn't care too much about all this grievance arbitration stuff. They care about what can the union do to

"To me, workers didn't care too much about all this grievance arbitration stuff. They care about what can the union do to help them, like providing housing, fighting for access to health care, helping with their eviction notices, or dealing with getting their phones shut off. Regular day-to-day, real-life issues."

In addition, it's not a factory. It's not a hospital, where all of us know that we are coming here today, and we are working under the same conditions, and we can change it. When we started to organize the workers, it was like 35,000 homecare workers identified in L.A. County. That's 35,000 worksites, households, different working conditions, and supervisors and clients.

We had to get people to understand that yes, this is a job. We had to explain: you have to do your hours, and social workers come out and approve your hours. It's funded by Medicaid and the state and the county. This is a job, and we can make a difference. We were having conversations with the providers about how they can help better their lives. Like all healthcare workers, homecare workers were interested in quality care. I think what goes across well to the providers, that I found when I was

help them, like providing housing, fighting for access to health care, helping with their eviction notices, or dealing with getting their phones shut off. Regular day-to-day, real-life issues. Getting their check on time—how do we get to the social worker to make sure the check gets to them on time so they can pay their bills? So it was the real bread-and-butter issues that they really cared about and wanted the union to help them with.

People were very serious about the union. We had nothing, very few union services, and no sign of getting a wage increase or health care or anything. But people were paying dues of $7.38 a month to the union just in hope, saying, "I believe in what the union is doing, and it can make a difference." Workers voluntarily paid union dues through checks or money orders until we were able to get deductions from the state. In the early stages, these activists were largely middle-aged African American women who built the union. They worked three or four jobs. They were working a lot. They had to make ends meet. When I started you had a lot of African American women. Today you have mostly Latinas, and you have a huge group that is in the San Fernando Valley, northwest of L.A., which is an Armenian and Russian group. Huge group, unbelievably large. I'd say the number one group is Latinas, then you have blacks, and Armenians and Russians.

The homecare campaign as a grassroots

make a phone call to whoever the elected official is, we would help them with just general information. We had this education about how can you do something to change what's happening in your community.

So we didn't just deal with homecare issues. I think that is part of why we were able to bring them back to the meeting to the union hall to be active and to call twenty-five or so homecare workers. The other thing we had to deal with was the geographical lines. Some members in South Central would not cross the 110 freeway, so we had to do a meeting over there and a

"People were very serious about the union. We had nothing, very few union services, and no sign of getting a wage increase or health care or anything. But people were paying dues of $7.38 a month to the union just in hope, saying, "I believe in what the union is doing, and it can make a difference." Workers voluntarily paid union dues through checks or money orders until we were able to get deductions from the state."

campaign evolved from the members. We mixed the traditional and nontraditional ways of doing things. We knocked on doors and talked to people. We did mass mailings after getting the list around neighbors and friends. We did a combination of a whole lot of different things to reach out to workers. We have a lot of those leaders still working, but one of the things that I noticed was that these women were very hungry to do something. There was not a lot of community involvement in their communities, and they saw the union as a way to get out there and speak about some of the things that went on in their communities. So we had meetings that weren't focused entirely on the union; they focused on what was going on in their communities, and we figured out how to help them. If they had to write a letter or

meeting over here, and we had to respect that. We had to understand what the whole landscape was.

I remember having coffee at McDonald's with ten leaders, and they would come and get their list, and they would go back and call, and we would have some of the biggest meetings. But then we would need a bigger hall to invite more people, so those leaders also helped us with locations, as they knew more about the community, and we would develop leaders from those in attendance. So yeah, we had a lot of homecare workers who were invested in making a difference.

We had members trained to do the marshal work for rallies. We had members trained to do the speaker's bureau so that we could go and make public comments at board meetings and Sacramento. We activated our members in very creative ways. One component that we used that was quite effective was, we broke the list of members down by assembly and senate districts. We would target different assembly and senate members, and if they were up for election, we would get our members in the respective districts to turn out and vote and make sure that the elected officials were committed to do something in Sacramento for our homecare workers. One of the highlights of that brought us closer to victory—I think it was at the 1996 Democratic National Convention. We did a video on homecare workers and consumers. You could hear a pin drop in that room. And that's when I think a lot of people started to get involved and asking, "How can I help?" Things started changing. The next governor, Gray Davis, was there, I remember, and Art Torres—a lot of people were there. It was just unbelievable. People wanted to do something about it.

By the end of 1996 everyone knew about the homecare workers. We had times when we were knocking on doors during the minimum wage fight and people would say, "Hey, we know exactly what you want, and we are on your side. We want it as much as you want it." It was unbelievable when we were walking through the state capitol, and everyone knew what we were fighting for, and they would listen to our story. We never had a time where elected officials were shutting doors or not wanting to hear what

"The homecare campaign had an enormous challenge: how to organize poor African American women working in isolated conditions. The campaign is one of the best examples of bringing together workers, consumers, and community groups."

we were saying. I think the mere fact that workers got on the bus and drove across the state for more than five hours to get to Sacramento—the elected officials wanted to talk about it because it was powerful. They took off from their jobs, leaving their houses and kids to travel for five hours. We were very serious and that was very important. I can't say that at that time we had any bad thing happen on any of the buses. The workers were happy. Even today you have some people that used to go that say, "Are you going back to Sacramento? I want to go!" because they had such a good experience there.

By the time we got recognition, the workforce had doubled to 74,000. After the union election in 1999, we got our first contract with the state, funding a fifty-cent increase. The following year we had to fight with the county to get funding. Then we started the union in a small, nontraditional way, without using reps, but using member services and a contract administration department, where we would do what reps do, but not on same level. We would figure out what the problems were, and how we could use member services to solve the problems and work with the social workers and the department of social services to solve problems. We didn't use the grievance procedure, where you have a certain amount of time to file leading up to arbitration.

The coalition component was another important part of the campaign. The homecare campaign organized consumers, community groups, Democrats and Republicans. During the campaign we were taught to look for the unusual suspect, people who generally wouldn't support this kind of campaign. So you move from trying to get everyone on board to get people that would not support us on board, to figure out how to win them over. Also, the research component is important. We had staff working with our International and universities to come up with white papers that supported the argument to unionize the workers.

The homecare campaign had an enormous challenge: how to organize poor African American women working in isolated conditions. The campaign is one of the best examples of bringing together workers, consumers, and community groups. Finally, we have a lot more work to do, as the numbers of workers are even higher now, about 115,000 in L.A. County and close to 400,000 statewide.

Kirk Adams

Kirk Adams, former campaign director.

Kirk Adams was campaign director of the homecare worker organizing campaign from 1987 to 1990. He managed strategy, budget, staff, and community and political relations. He is currently the executive director of SEIU Healthcare Division, overseeing all of SEIU national healthcare organizing projects.

Before I came to SEIU, I worked for this very small, independent union called the United Labor Unions, which Mark Splain and I both worked for.[1] We organized about five homecare agencies in Boston. It certainly was the first connect I had with homecare workers, the first sense about some of the things people raise when you say homecare workers: "Oh, they don't work together? How could you possibly have a union when people aren't in the same workplace?" You realize that was all a bunch of bull, because basically there

> *"L.A. taught us we had to find the right construct to do this, and that's all about politics of one sort or another."*

was a huge community of interest here and very, very committed folks. We went on strike, in fact. We struck them in Boston. We didn't strike the clients; we struck the agency. It's not really a linguistic thing. The way we did it was we actually provided the service to the client, but because you didn't put it on your timesheets, the agency couldn't collect the money from the state.

Then ultimately we took the worker and convinced the client to go to another agency. So we really put some economic pressure on them. We actually won that strike, but it certainly showed that from the standpoint of workers—this has been consistent throughout—there was a strong identity, sense of community, sense of "we want to work, not only to improve our situation, but the situation of the system for the consumers." That was my first take on that. That was in 1981, I guess.

In the initial campaign in Los Angeles, I was the director of the campaign as lead organizer. I don't remember the exact title I had back then. It was a project campaign that SEIU decided to do in Los Angeles, in the sense that it was targeting in-home providers as opposed to agency homecare workers, which had not been done. It was going to try to do it in a way that either challenged the legal status or looked at it in a variety of different ways. It was a specific idea, strategy, campaign that the International Union decided to invest in and fund. It was a decision at that time by two names you'll know, John Sweeney and Andy Stern, based on really a proposal that I developed, which was based on, again, past experience in organizing homecare workers and relationships that I had and really having a discussion with another person, Mark Splain, who is the health care organizing director at SEIU.[2]

At the time, we had finished certain campaigns—the Beverly Nursing Home Campaign, at least that phase of it.[3] I was looking for the next phase. There were a variety of different places I could have

"I think the grassroots organizing was important to build the organization, to build an identity both among homecare workers and among the general public and the decision makers and the general public. We needed to go to a political movement."

turned, left, right, or center, and L.A. was the one we spent some time on looking at, doing some research on. Then there was a meeting at Saint Louis. I remember that we, Mark and I, talked to Andy about doing this and got the green light to go out and begin to some degree. Although we knew it was a huge number of workers, we didn't know how big it was. We didn't know very much about what it would actually be at the end of the day. It made sense, because at the time Andy wanted to export organizing talent to Los Angeles anyway. And so my wife, Cecile, was exported to Local 399 at the time to be the organizing director. I was exported to do this homecare exploration. For SEIU, they had a lot of internal reasons even if the homecare thing had never happened in some respects. They wanted to put folks in Southern California. So there's a lot of background to it.

The summer of 1987 was when we really did a lot of research, outreach, and began to create the structure under which we could do this—which at the time was 434, ultimately it became 434B—developed some of the legal theories, developed some of the mapping of the situation. It wasn't until October of 1987 that we formally kicked off the campaign based on a theory that, if we signed up a huge number of these folks and filed under Meyers-Milias-Brown—a local government bargaining law—we would force the issue.[4] We knew the county and the state would not just back off, and we thought we'd take it to court and win.

October seventeenth, I believe—the way you can figure this out is that it's the day that the stock market fell like five hundred points. I know we did a meeting once and really went through a process because of Meyers-Milias-Brown Act's requirements that you collect—I forget now, but I think it was 20 percent cards from the workers. But you had to collect it within ninety days, and so we really did have this huge outreach going on from the middle of October through December, and filed in January. We collected twenty-two thousand cards, and then we went to court. Then the court said no.

I think what the county was thinking all along was two things. One is that the state would foot the bill, there was going to be a division of responsibility, a division of, particularly, the cost. That's where the county and us got edgewise. I think they were thinking that at some point, the legal process would finger the state as the funder, which they were for all intents and purposes. At the end of the line, when we got more serious six years later, there was the issue of how much the county would be responsible for. There are other issues too. It was after I left, so I wouldn't know all the ins and outs, but there was a fair amount of political tension on the County Board of Supervisors about even just the relationship with SEIU and why they would or would not support this. It has become much more as we've gone through this negotiation cycle, just the stress of public funding of this deal, and the state and the county competing with each other about who's going to get stuck with the biggest chunk here. Or how big a chunk would the county get stuck with. The state always knew they had the

majority interest, but there's this issue of 65–35 percent versus 75–25 percent, which didn't seem like a huge amount of money, but it is a huge amount of money. They continued to say the county and the state have certain employee responsibilities, but collective bargaining is not one of them. So that put us back in Nowheresville.

We had at the time signed up a huge number of folks by card-check, which were dues deduction cards.[5] We had to go back to the 22,000 or so folks and get them to support the dues deductions. I think it was like 14,000. We were spending a huge amount of money on this campaign to keep it together. I think really at that point two things happened. One, the question of, could we sustain this organization without collective bargaining for a period of time? That put us in the direction of talking to Mr. Gray Davis, who was the controller. The reason we wanted to talk to Gray Davis is because he oversaw the payroll of homecare workers. And he could grant the right to do dues deductions. One, we had to figure out how to sustain the organization through dues deductions. The second, we had to decide on the collective bargaining strategy, which was the Public Authority. To move forward with establishing an entity for collective bargaining, we knew establishing a Public Authority to be that entity was essential. We looked at it, thought about it, had it on the shelf there, but really couldn't move it until we had the politics better. The Public Authority was really the theory that now has really got us where we are today. But looking back, it took a while for the campaign to get to that final policy hurdle. We needed to get the politics right. By that I mean not only the legislative gubernatorial issues but the politics with the consumers and other stakeholders almost before we even talked to workers.

I think the grassroots organizing was important to build the organization, to build an identity both among homecare workers and among the general public and the decision makers and the general public. We needed to go to a political movement. Even though I came into that campaign later, people might give me a little credit for appreciating the consumer role here. There was not a huge amount of consumer contact with folks in the first six months of this campaign. It was all worker-driven and somewhat ally-driven—the African American community, the African American ministers—but other than that, we didn't have consumers on board. It's never been an issue about the workers. We've never lost a homecare worker; well, I think we lost a couple—I don't know why—but very few.

We have to talk to workers, because you have to create a grassroots organization. But we spent literally millions of dollars talking to all the workers, and we really only needed to talk to a small percentage of them to get some legitimacy, because the workers will come if the issue is right. Through homecare, we created an organizing model that is very much more cost-efficient in terms of getting it done. We spent all this money to talk to workers. In the case of Washington state, we thought there were 14,000 workers, and there ended up being 26,000. Every time we've looked at these things, we've always underestimated what the number was. L.A. taught us we had to find the right construct to do this, and that's all about politics of one sort or another. Whether it's Oregon or Washington or Illinois or now New Jersey

Kirk Adams (left) at a Los Angeles rally in 1995.

and other places, it's just been a question of, can we get the politics right.

I think in L.A. once we realized we were in for a long fight, we said this had to be broader than just workers' interest. From that point of view, we settled down and said we had to come to terms with folks who get the services, because not only could they be a huge help here, but they can kill us. They can say this is bad for them. Some of them felt that way at the outset. More from just concerns and fear and lack of knowledge about unions or lack of knowledge about what this was going to look like. We began this outreach to folks primarily on the disabled side, less so on the senior side because they had the biggest questions.

The biggest were raised by the independent living movement in California. To that degree, the only one of the real advantages I had was that in Texas, while organizing nursing homes, where I had worked a long time, I met this guy named Bob Kafka, who runs ADAPT [American Disabled for Attendant Programs Today]. ADAPT for years has been a disabled advocate. Bob hates nursing homes. He would do anything to burn them all down if he could. We met and talked a number of times, and he's really a remarkable guy. He did say to me, which I remember, he said, "Kirk, you're sort of missing the point here. It isn't about the workers. It's about the workers and the consumers here. If you understood that, not only would you be right," by what he defines as being right, "but you'd be more effective."

He was right, whether it is nursing homes or any of this stuff. That's really the start of that discussion, which started a little bumpy. We made certain mistakes, but in all, it didn't take that much to get people to really appreciate that this could maybe work in terms of what a common ground was, eliminating all these fears or ideological issues, and we began to develop a coalition that ultimately was a very powerful coalition in Sacramento. It helped us a huge amount with the L.A. Board of Supervisors, too, because of their problems with SEIU. So just having them as a partner was a huge advantage.

Historically, I think we, the labor movement, have been ad hoc, or episodic, or whatever you want to say, about coalition building. We only do it when we need it, and once we don't need it, we step out of it and go away. In this case in California, I think people, certainly the advocates, said, "We're not going to get into this just to win something for you all. We have our agenda, so you have to commit to our agenda. And our agenda includes these, these, these." Unless there's real vested interest here, these things don't survive. People go and do their own business. So we had to be central to their business, and they had to be central to ours. We knew they were central to ours. We just had to get central to theirs in terms of really producing for them. There are some organizational reasons to do it; there were also some political reasons to do it.

There's no question, though, that the homecare workers could not have won this without SEIU's political muscle. This is not 74,000 homecare workers. It's about 300,000 SEIU members in California and the political contributions, the political turnout, the political relationships that SEIU has in the legislature primarily and then hopefully in the governor's office. This was really, again, what I think the advocates and others, the consumers, saw, was that SEIU was willing to put the political muscle, the whole union, even the international union, in play here to win things that were important to them. And that's why it's a valuable, or real, partnership. Now when we go and talk to people in Michigan about organizing in Michigan, the disabled community there, they had the usual list of issues. But it was a much easier conversation, because they picked up the phone and talked to people in California that said not only is this okay, it's not going to hurt you, but it can be a huge advantage to you in terms of getting things done. This is real political muscle here, as opposed to the crumbs that you guys get from walking around the halls of this capitol. So it accelerated the process, eliminated the timeline that it took to build that relationship, so it was a huge advantage. When people get up and say bad things about us, we had folks to vouch for us.

I think in California, because the politics have gone our way for awhile, I think we have been a good partner in producing things that they wanted, and they've certainly been a good partner with us in terms of things we wanted. It's just been a fact of life that whenever you make a partnership, it isn't all about your deal; it's about the other side's deal, and you have to be really ready to expend political chips to get their deal done. Even people like the national leadership of the disabled community, Bob Kafka, and other folks have vouched for us, too. I think it's something we had to learn in our dealings not only with those folks but with the African American community, with the Latino community. Unless we get into their issues, they're not going to get into ours. So we're better partners.

The grassroots thing was actually incredibly helpful in terms of building an organization—efforts to raise the minimum wage and policy changes, specifically legislation to get the Public Authority. The third one was the coalition campaigns. So even though we knew we were in this dead-end alley here after the case was lost, even with appeals, by going into these grassroots issues we got some breaks in terms of this minimum wage, thing coming up. We found out that we could organize and build an organization around these issues. Homecare workers would rally around them; they would take the time, spend the money, go through all the demonstrations—we were not simply just reaching out to workers about the union. We saw these issues would get workers on buses to Sacramento.

Some people would do a deeper analysis of the homecare workers union. You could say a significant portion of people are family members to these people; they don't even see it as a job. That wasn't even my question. It wasn't about, do they see it as a job. The

question was, do they see it as worth their time to fight for something. Even if they were family members, they clearly did, in some respects even more so. It was like a double hit for them. It has in some respects informed us in terms of the structure that we're building for homecare workers. It certainly told us that this is a different type of organizing. It's more like community organizing. You're basically getting people organized to go after their money, and the money in most cases is up there at the state capitol. That's what it is. It isn't about work rules; it isn't about any of the traditional labor issues that come into play. From that regard, we could toss those away, which was helpful in terms of dealing with disabilities advocates. It also frankly has changed how we organize. After fifty years of fighting the nursing home industry, we've gone to this model, too. I mean that's really the biggest lesson out of California was to get the politics right.

It also made us see this issue as far more than a union worker issue. It wasn't just about political power, or the worker's interest, or even the consumer's. It actually makes public policy sense, basing care in the home. That's the other part of our deal here that has been helpful: that we can talk about this as very strong public policy that politicians could talk about publicly to everybody. They didn't have to say, "Oh, I'm doing this for the union," or they didn't have to say, "I'm doing this for the wheelchair folks." "I'm doing this because it makes budget sense, makes lots of sense."

Our analysis is that we're heading for a crisis here, a huge crisis, because of the aging of America. The funding system as it's now created will go into cardiac arrest here sometime in the next ten years. It doesn't matter who's in office. If they want to keep their jobs, they're going to have to figure out a way to do this, because it's not like health care, where they can say, "Well, actually, the people who don't have health care don't vote, I don't have to worry." This is their dirty little secret here. It's not so much a secret anymore. But this is totally about Americans who vote, and they are parents in themselves. And they are going to be knocking on somebody's door and saying, "This is just not going to cut it. Either I'm going broke, or the care is shitty, or something's wrong here, and somebody better respond here." People see long-term care, because of Medicaid, as a public responsibility, not as a private responsibility. It's just a shifting of priorities. It takes money, but there's a better way to do it. There is a huge amount of inefficiency in the system. So it's not always about just throwing money into the nursing home industry, for instance. There is a better way to deliver this stuff. Homecare is a cheaper, better way to do this. So that has to be taken from where it still is—and that is second-class status—and put into an overall delivery system. People are going to get older in America, and the system that now is there will be totally overwhelmed. There's no question about that. Everybody agrees on that. People just don't agree on what to do about it.

Notes

1. Mark Splain is currently a special assistant in the AFL-CIO's Department of Organizing, working with and assisting the organizing efforts of the United Farm Workers (UFW). See http://organizersforum.org/index.php?id=352.
2. Andy Stern, a labor leader and activist, is currently president of SEIU. See http//:www.seiu.org/about/officers_bios/stern_bio.cfm.
3. Beverly Nursing Home Campaign was a campaign to organize Beverly Nursing Home workers.
4. The Meyers-Milias-Brown Act is a law that regulates labor-management relationships in California's cities, counties, and most special districts. See http://c[er.berkely.edu/pocketguide/guide5.html.
5. Card check is an organizing method in which employers agree to recognize a union if the union presents signed authorization forms, or cards, from a majority of the workers.

David Rolf

David Rolf, about 2004.

David Rolf directed the homecare worker organizing campaign from 1995 to 1999. He is the president of SEIU 775NW, which represents over 30,000 homecare and nursing home workers across Washington state.

The public authority structure created bargaining rights. Without the authority, we didn't have a legal mechanism to create a legal union for the 74,000 workers to get the ability to bargain for better wages and working conditions. In the traditional union setting, the defined employer is responsible for hiring, firing, working conditions, covering people under workers' compensation, deducting taxes, etc. One thing under federal labor law is the right to negotiate with an employer if workers vote to create a union. Bargaining subjects are generally around wages, hours, and conditions. Here's the situation in Los Angeles: county social workers set the hours, county government set the wages, and working conditions were set by the consumer. When we attempted to get the county or state to respect working conditions, they wouldn't take responsibility for being the employer. In 1991, a court of law agreed with them, not with us. The public authority answered the legal questions of who is the employer of record for purposes of collective bargaining. Authority has other functions from the union standpoint. In statute it was an option for counties to create a legal structure to facilitate collective bargaining.

The authority model was really the result of political compromise between unions, senior citizens groups, disability rights groups, state and local governments. The interest of the various participants could be described this way: SEIU wanted a means by which to organize tens and later hundreds of thousands of workers to bargain for wages and benefits. Seniors and other consumer advocates thought of ways of offering registries and background checks and reducing worker turnover. Disability rights organizations wanted to preserve the consumer-directed model of homecare, where their rights to hire, discipline, or fire the workers and control the workplace couldn't be controlled by the union or the government. Local government was interested in making incremental improvements in working conditions, but cautious about increasing costs and very cautious, because of the cost they thought it might incur, about taking on a direct role as employer. State government at the time was generally opposed to creating a statewide bargaining organization. The legislation would let local governments opt in to create public authorities at the county level.

The political compromise resulting from this collision of interests created the first version of the authority model. It was enacted in 1993 and implemented in 1994 to 2000. Under the model, SEIU and workers got a bargaining law that gave them a method to organize workers county to county, with an important caveat. We had to get counties to agree. It was an option. Later on, [Governor] Wilson signed legislation to remove the option. Beginning in 2000, [counties] had to adopt some employer-of-record structure for their homecare workers. Also, in the compromise senior citizen organizations gained a promise of improved services through a registry, background checks, training for workers, and promises of reduced turnover as wages and benefits improved. Disability rights organizations won what amounted to a statutory prohibition on union interference on the rights of consumers to hire, fire, and supervise workers. They won a promise by the union never to conduct a strike. And insurance from elected officials that their ability to control what goes on in their home would remain safe. County governments could choose to create public authorities, but without any mandated increased costs unless counties voluntarily agreed to them. The state government incurred no obligations to serve as employer.

> "SEIU wanted a means by which to organize tens and later hundreds of thousands of workers to bargain for wages and benefits."

The Public Authority that was created in the early '90s and not adopted in L.A. until 1997 was absolutely the result of political compromise where a number of orgs had to give something to get something. It was also highly imperfect. If it were the union's sole choice we wouldn't want to give up the right to make a claim on state and county budgets. We would leave it up to politicians acting alone. I think that if we had it to do over again, it would be preferable to have a statewide union, instead of a different contract in every county. And I'm sure that there are many county Boards of Supervisors throughout California and I'm sure Governor Wilson would rather have never heard of this idea to begin with. The point really about all this is we didn't start out dreaming about the Public Authority as the solution for homecare; it really was a practical, real-life compromise between the various stakeholders within the IHSS program.

Partnership for Dignity and Survival

"It is not how much you do, but how much love you put in the doing."

— Mother Theresa

Homecare workers and their clients form human bonds that create a partnership intertwined with dignity, respect, and, more often than not, love. The Los Angeles homecare organizing campaign made clear that homecare workers and their clients work in coalition to provide better lives for both provider and consumer. From bathing to feeding, housekeeping to medicating, homecare workers are a lifeline. In this section we explore this special relationship.

Joyce Hayashi

Joyce Hayashi.

Joyce Hayashi provides care for her sister and mother. She has been an activist and homecare worker for many years. She is a member of the executive board and is a trustee of the union's health trust.

I became a homecare worker when my mother suffered a severe stroke that left her completely incapacitated. It was quite bad. That was in January of 1993. My sister Doreen, who is sitting next to me, unfortunately has muscular dystrophy, and so I became responsible for both my mother and sister. When my mother became initially ill, it wasn't easy, of course. She went through about six months of rehabilitative care, in and out of nursing homes and a rehab. The rehab center then was at Daniel Freeman Hospital. They had a wonderful rehab center there, and her neurologist sent her there, and they did a great job—enough to get her back

home. She was on a G-tube, which was an intestinal feeding tube. And they were able to at least get her to eat pureed foods.

Doreen was less incapacitated fifteen years ago than she is now, because muscular dystrophy is a progressive disease, and they trained both of us to care for our mother at home. We were both working full-time at the time of my mother's stroke, and it necessitated Doreen to go part-time and me as well. Eventually I couldn't sustain my position. I was operational vice president of a production company, and I wasn't able to maintain that position. I made the choice to take care of both my mother and sister and gave up work. So it was financially very difficult as well as physically difficult and, of course, emotionally. A few years later, when we did apply for in-home support service because we had spent down all of our savings—a combined savings of my mother, myself, and my sister—we got a few hours to get assistance. We did that, and we figured it out that between Doreen and I, we were getting paid $1.77 an hour. That's the kind of sacrifice that families make when they decide to take care of family members and loved ones. It's a 24/7 job.

Usually the person that a homecare worker is caring for is either quite elderly and/or disabled. So then that means that all of their living functions have to be taken care of. That begins with the personal care, which is feeding, cooking, bathing, and if a person is incontinent like my mother is, that includes all of that and the laundry and dealing with that on a twenty-four-hour basis, because the body breaks down if you don't reposition a person every two hours. Then administratively, you need to take care of their financial affairs, their banking, paying their bills for them, seeing that they have a decent place to live and the conditions are comfortable for them. So if anything breaks down in the house, you have to make sure that that's taken care of. For instance, my mother's heater went out; we had to get that redone. You have to make sure that all of those kinds of things are satisfactory.

If there's any rehabilitation work that goes on, usually you have to do that yourself. So for me, it entailed taking my mother

"We did that, and we figured it out that between Doreen and I, we were getting paid $1.77 an hour. That's the kind of sacrifice that families make when they decide to take care of family members and loved ones. It's a 24/7 job."

to a wonderful program at Santa Monica College, called Pathfinders, and they helped her regain some of her physical abilities, which unfortunately have diminished again just because of age. She is now approaching eighty-six years old. But we still continue to do rehabilitative exercises with her to keep her muscle tone and keep the spasm out of her body, which is something that stroke victims suffer from. If left unattended, they will curl up into a position and not be able to come out of it again, and that's uncomfortable for everyone. You can hardly move a patient that's paralyzed, and they can't do anything with themselves. So that's a constant that had to be done; then there are also cognitive exercises that you have to maintain, making the effort to get the patient to talk, to get my mother to talk. And stroke patients for some reason are able to sing more than they can talk, so we do a lot of singing with her and tongue exercises, the whole range of things just to keep her healthy; then there's the arranging for her doctors, getting her to her physicians and making sure she has all of the medications. I didn't even mention doing the laundry or cleaning the house. Somewhere out there, you do it in your sleep.

I never actually believed or thought I would be a homecare worker. It was nothing that I ever envisioned at all. And in fact, that is probably the same dynamic that happens in most families, that they just are not expecting this to happen. They go about their lives, and suddenly some family member, some parent, becomes ill, and a crisis occurs, and they have to deal

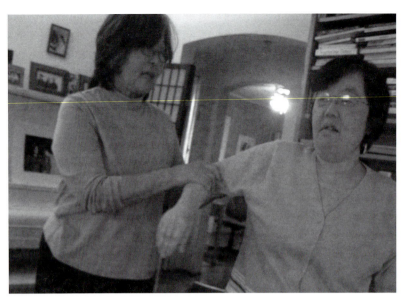
Joyce Hayashi helping her sister, Doreen Hayashi at their Santa Monica home, 2007.

for ten years when I heard about the union. I may have received something in the mail telling me about it. And so, other than that, I really had no other information about the union, mainly because I think most of the homecare workers in the union are in central Los Angeles, and this is way out on the coast. I don't think there are many homecare workers out in Santa Monica and Venice. But I must have gotten some sort of information through the mail, and it had information about the local meeting, and that's how I first became connected with the union. So I went to a

with it. I think that most people now prefer aging in place. They would like to stay in their homes. I think enough publicity has been made available about some of the deficiencies of nursing care in convalescent homes. I am not saying anything against them because they serve a vital function,

"The union has been instrumental in uplifting both wages and benefits for homecare workers. It hasn't been tremendous, but it's been steady, and I know all homecare workers appreciate it. They appreciate having a voice in the system, because we do tremendous work."

and a great many patients need just that kind of care. But a lot of patients who have access to fairly good health care and have aged well can stay at home. It's better for them, it's better for their families, and certainly economically and politically, it's a better solution, because nursing homes are tremendously expensive. I think when you weigh that against maybe the benefits that they provide for the majority of aging and disabled patients, it's a better solution to stay at home.

I had already been a homecare worker

divisional meeting. The union has meetings in their different counties, and they encourage members to go there monthly to find out what's going on with the union, what's happening politically, and what they need to do to move things along.

So I went to one of these meetings five years ago and from there, I volunteered to work in one of the committees, and about a year later I was elected to the executive board as a divisional vice president. And I served on that board for about three years until we went statewide last November, and we eliminated vice presidents because we are now covering all of California. So I am a board member along with fifty other members from the state.

The union has been instrumental in uplifting both wages and benefits for homecare workers. It hasn't been tremendous, but it's been steady, and I know all homecare workers appreciate it. They appreciate having a voice in the system, because we do tremendous work. I don't think it's simply about wages and benefits. The mission, I believe, of the homecare union—and I should clarify that, because it's a long-term care workers' union, because we represent nursing homes and convalescent homes as well—our mission is to lift homecare workers out of poverty, and so that's more than wages and benefits. We have a housing trust, and we are involved in building homes for long-term care workers, providing financing so that they can move up to home ownership and work themselves out of poverty. We also have a health care trust, of which I am privileged to be a trustee, and we have provided health care to many workers in counties throughout California who have not previously had health care. There's a nominal fee. It's quite reasonable when you think about what you hear in the news about both employers and employees paying hundreds of dollars every month. Our trust is able to provide low-cost health care, which includes both vision and dental as well as providing for a new system for several counties, which allows patients to reach physicians by phone. And this is really important to homecare workers in rural areas in California who don't have easy access to a health provider. So we make health care accessible to all health care workers regardless of the number of hours that they work. Because usually policies require that homecare workers work at least eighty hours.

We estimate that we now represent more than 150,000 homecare workers. As the population ages, there's going to be more and more need for homecare workers. I have friends who often call me who say, "Joyce, can you help me with this? I know you've been taking care of your mother and your sister for a long time, and now my mother is having problems, etc. What can I do?" And I do explain to them that they can seek help from the union. And I also tell them about in-home support service, the other end as well, and how they can contact them and get information. I know that we have a website that can be accessed by the public. We do a great deal of publicity in local newspapers, primarily when we're asking for support. But it seems to me that those ads are also geared toward letting the public know that this union does exist in their city.

Doreen Hayashi

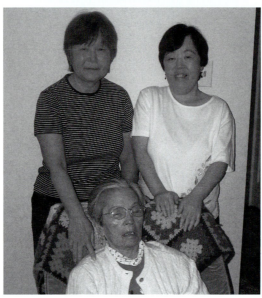

Joyce Hayashi (left) cares for her sister Doreen Hayashi and their mother May, 2007.

Doreen Hayashi helped her sister Joyce care for their mother until she became disabled by myotonic muscular dystrophy. Joyce is now Doreen's homecare provider as well.

I became familiar with homecare when my sister involved me in her activities at the union. This was while the two of us were caring for our mother, who suffered a massive stroke. I was working full-time, five days a week, at an office as a receptionist. I was working full-time and taking care of my mother, and that's just too much for one person, basically. It's like having two jobs with nonstop activities. But while taking care of my mother, along with Joyce, I noticed my health began to change.

"If there was research done, I bet it would show that people would not be as well as they are without the homecare workers and the union's help in training them."

It was 1999 when I was diagnosed with myotonic muscular dystrophy, not knowing it was hereditary. It began to progress more and more. Eventually I became disabled and unable to work at my job, and it was difficult to help with the care of my mother.

So having to know that I have this disease is rather depressing, but I've functioned very well dealing with it. I've been able to have my sister's help, which has meant a whole lot. She does most everything for me. She does all the shopping, all the cooking, and all house cleaning. She does the laundry, the dishes, takes out the trash, sets up appointments. She does everything. Then increasingly, she's having to do more and more. I know I can't do certain things physically that I could before, like squatting to sit down and picking myself up, so she helps me do that. Sometimes she holds me when I'm walking, just simple little things like that. She has helped me, because I am not able to do it. Opening containers, I can't do that, my grip is so bad, so I always have my sister open this and start this and pour that, so whatever has to be done. And she does this also for my mother. We have the help of Norma, another homecare worker, but it is a lot on Joyce's shoulders.

At the beginning, I was a homecare worker along with my sister, and now I've become a person who needs homecare. It was a necessity. To need this kind of care is very difficult. There is no way you can say, "Well, I know how you feel." Don't say that to me. Because it is a very painful and sometimes depressing place to be in. My girlfriend's mother had the same problem. She was there talking about my mother. She didn't understand it; then her mother suffered a stroke, and she talked to me all about it. And I said, "Carol, I know. Don't tell me; I know how hard it is." So in my case, it was a necessity to just go with the flow and just try to change your role. There were no questions about it. Joyce has decided to care for me and my mother. Because of our family, she had to make that choice. There is no question; she had to. I could not live without the support of my sister. She does everything for me. I would not be in this good a condition without her help, without her being here and helping me do other things, helping me with decisions on things

> "But for those family members that do make the choice to give up their own lives to care for a family member, they give up their jobs, their livelihood, everything, and they should have some dignity. And because this is, now, what Joyce does day in and day out, she deserves to have good wages and health benefits."

that I have problems with, just doing things for me. I couldn't cope without her. It's a decision every family is going to face. Some families are very close, and some others may not want to sacrifice everything to take care of their family members. Some people just don't want responsibility, so they just don't take care of them. I know a lot of people at my workplace that do that, because taking care of a person takes a lot of time.

But for those family members that do make the choice to give up their own lives to care for a family member, they give up their jobs, their livelihood, everything, and they should have some dignity. And because this is, now, what Joyce does day in and day out, she deserves to have good wages and health benefits. She focuses on the whole family now. It can be very stressful. It comes directly from her to me and my mother. As I grow older, I will need homecare for the rest of my life. The doctors say I would not be as well as I am without my sister's help. They say my nutrition, my diet, is why things have not progressed into a worse situation. I owe that to my sister. If there was research done, I bet it would show that people would not be as well as they are without the homecare workers and the union's help in training them.

Annie Mae Turner

Annie Mae Turner with Laurene Mackey, 2007.

Annie Mae Turner has been a homecare client for over twenty years and Laurene Mackey's client for ten years.

I'm from Alabama. I came out here in 1958. I'm eighty-six, looking at eighty-seven. I have a niece and nephew out here, but I have some nieces and nephews back in Alabama—no sisters, no brothers, just a niece and nephew, a couple of sisters-in-law. I have one son. My son is in the hospital. He's been in the hospital going on ten years now. He's in a nursing home. He had a stroke. He can't walk either. I worked until 1976, and then I retired. I had arthritis, where my legs and arms swelled. The people I worked for moved, and I didn't want to go up there with them. I was a cook. I broke my leg in 1986. When I broke my leg, my son was living here with me; he worked for me. Then my niece worked for me. Then my nephew worked for me. Then another girl worked for me. That girl is in a nursing home now.

Then the next one I got was Mrs. Mackey. I don't know how she's stayed with me. She's still with me. Mrs. Mackey's my provider. I think she's worked for me maybe about ten years. She comes over and helps me do everything. I still cook sometimes; I make people's cakes. I don't cook like I used to, because my son's

> "I'm just glad I have somebody to talk to, somebody to call me, check on me."

not here. I just cook for myself when Mrs. Mackey doesn't cook for me. I can get myself dressed; I just can't get in the tub. She's a very good provider. She's very nice and intelligent. She thinks of others more than herself sometimes. She calls every day. If she has to go to the union or something in the morning, she'll go there and then come back here. We get along just fine. We don't have arguments or anything. We just don't have disagreements. We understand each other.

People don't help you all the time like people used to when I came along. People would come out of the fields and go cook for sick people. Somebody wants to do something for me, I thank them. I appreciate it and enjoy it. If they enjoy it, I enjoy it, too. I don't get lonely. Everybody gets depressed sometimes. I'm not getting lonely. I've had my day. I don't have anything to get lonely about. I'm just glad I have somebody to talk to, somebody to call me, check on me, and see about me. I thank God for that. I thank God for all of his goodness. He brought me from a long way.

Laurene Mackey

Laurene Mackey (right) with a team of homecare workers at the Los Angeles local, about 2002.

Laurene Mackey managed a small family business for many years before she retired and became a homecare worker. She is a member of the executive board for SEIU Local 6434. She provides care for Annie Mae Turner.

've been doing this work a long time, but I wasn't getting paid for it all the time. I took care of my mother and my father; they were sick. Then I took care of my two aunties when they were sick. I owned a cleaners. I had a cleaners all my life. I opened at seven, and then I closed at seven. I was there every day. My husband got sick, and then he passed. My kids all went to college. Then I said, there's no sense in me working like this. I accomplished everything. I sent them to school, and they got their education. They're out making good money. So why should I have this cleaners? So I sold it. I think I sold that cleaners about in 1986. I couldn't get it out of my blood though.

> "It's just a thing where you have a tender feeling for people that can't help themselves."

I started working doing people's clothes out there in Hollywood, all those movie stars and things. Every time I passed a cleaners, I'd be looking at it. I said, now calm down. You've got to do better than this. You've got to find you something else to do.

Then I began to take care of people that couldn't take care of themselves. After that, I got with the union. I go down to the union a lot and do volunteer work. When they find one that'll work, they call them all the time. I slowed down one time with the union, after they called me all the time to come do something. I was going to take my rest. I was going to slow down. I like to cook, myself. I would sit there, and I would cook. I'd be eating my breakfast, saying, now what am I going to fix for dinner? I'd get up and fix it. Nobody was there but me. I'm eating dinner. I go take something out of the freezer to cook

"I would hate to just sit in the house with nobody coming to see me, nobody to talk to. That's what it takes in life, somebody to have somebody to talk to and care for them. You need people to be around, to care for you, take you different places, and do things for you, laugh, talk . . . and fuss too!"

for my lunch. So all of a sudden, I got high blood and got high cholesterol. I would go from the couch to the icebox eating, because I didn't have anything else to do. That's how I know it's very important that you get up and do things.

You just can't sit around and not do anything. I said, oh no, give me the union. I'm going back. I came by to see about Mrs. Turner, and I went back to the union, started back to work. So I started by coming over here helping her; then down to the union I'd go. Mrs. Turner has led a beautiful life. I sang solo sometimes at her church. My uncle introduced us. She plays the piano, and maybe I would sing for her sometimes. We met and from there, we've just been going on. I take her to the doctor. Sometimes I take her out to eat, and then I'll take her to the park, somewhere where she can have some kind of recreation. Because sitting at home all the time is not good. I come over and see about her. I do everything I can, because we are very important people with a very important job, taking care of the people who can't take care of themselves.

I thank God I can get around and take care of everything. I look at people my age and say, Lord, have mercy! I thank you for the blessing that you have given me. I'm seventy-eight. You see them out sometimes;

they need help. People just walk over them and don't pay them attention. Somebody will have to help me one day. My mother and father were in Texas. They were doing alright. The people I saw here, they needed help, and I would help them. I said, maybe somebody would help my parents, too. It's just a thing where you have a tender feeling for people that can't help themselves. It's so many of them being abused. I often think about my brother. My brother was sick. I tried to get him up here where I could take care of him. His kids wouldn't let him come. They put him in a home. I went over there one time, and he was crying. He said, "Why would my kids put me here?" He didn't live but six months after they put him there. That really did bother me. Boy, if my nieces would have let us have him, my brother would still be alive today. See, when you put them in a home, you put them there to die. They don't want to go into a home. All them that I can help, I'll do it.

I think what makes people live longer is when they enjoy themselves, when they have someone to talk to. I used to put together a bus trip for senior citizens. I would take them to the casinos. Now you are talking about somebody enjoying themselves, they really did enjoy that. They have to have something to look forward to. I would hate to just sit in the house with nobody coming to see me, nobody to talk to. That's what it takes in life, somebody to have somebody to talk to and care for them. You need people to be around, to care for you, take you different places, and do things for you, laugh, talk... and fuss too!

Moments in the Movement

"This is how change happens, though. It is a relay race, and we're very conscious of that, that our job really is to do our part of the race, and then we pass it on, and then someone picks it up, and it keeps going. And that is how it is. And we can do this, as a planet, with the consciousness that we may not get it, you know, today, but there's always a tomorrow."

— Alice Walker, BBC radio interview, 2008

Throughout the years, homecare workers overcame many obstacles to achieve success; these successes are recorded in the following timeline. Although it is difficult to capture every milestone of this important struggle, we present significant events of the Los Angeles County homecare campaign from 1987 to 2007. The timeline follows the path that homecare workers took to successfully unionize, obtain a contract, and build power for workers in the twenty-first century.

Moments in the Movement
Twenty Years of Homecare Organizing

SEIU members celebrate at the Black History Parade in Pasadena.

SEPTEMBER 1987
SEIU begins to organize homecare workers in Los Angeles County. Homecare workers start meeting and talking about forming a union.

DECEMBER 1987
Hundreds of homecare workers rally at the Los Angeles County Board of Supervisors meeting. Local 434 demands that the county supervisors raise the minimum wage from $3.75 to $4.75 per hour. The county supervisors agree and increase homecare workers' wages, effective June 1988.

Local 434B files a lawsuit against Los Angeles County asking the court to declare homecare workers as county employees since the county processes the timesheets, sets clients' hours, and supervises and administers the program.

Pamela Hall and Fred Lyons at member reporter training in San Bernardino.

JANUARY 1988
Union members deliver over 12,000 cards to Los Angeles County administration offices and demand union recognition.

The union holds its founding convention and establishes the structure for the Los Angeles Homecare Workers' Union.

Verdia Daniels participating in a demonstration for homecare workers, about 1999, Los Angeles.

MARCH–JUNE 1988
The union holds a series of demonstrations and demands improvement of the payroll system and an end to late checks.

The union holds rallies and demonstrations to demand that Los Angeles County officially recognize the union and begin negotiations on wages and benefits.

"This was an exploited work group because homecare workers were essentially independent contractors and unorganized. Without organizing and representation anything could be done to them. I felt it was a gross unfairness. The bill that I introduced said that the workers were employees of the county since it was the county who paid them. The counties were being short-sighted. These workers saved the government millions of dollars because it is cheaper to  treat someone in the home than to warehouse them in a nursing facility."

— Rod Wright, member of the California State Assembly

Los Angeles County and the union reach an agreement on a plan to improve the homecare system. The plan calls for the establishment of a registry to assist clients and providers, health care insurance for homecare workers, a wage increase, and annual contract negotiations.

LOCAL 434B
SEIU
Stronger Together

Local 434B logo.

OCTOBER 1988
The union is chartered and becomes the Los Angeles Homecare Workers' Union, SEIU Local 434B.

JANUARY 1989
The state refuses to fund the settlement agreed upon by Los Angeles County and Local 434B. Local 434B files a lawsuit against the state.

Governor George Deukmejian proposes a $64 million cut in the In-Home Supportive Service (IHSS) program.

FEBRUARY 1989
A judge rules that the county is not the sole employer of homecare workers but also disagrees that the client is the employer. The union appeals the decision to the Superior Court.

MARCH–JUNE 1989
Homecare workers—along with their clients, senior advocates, and members of the disabled community—hold demonstrations and testify in various legislative committees.

Governor Deukmejian announces full funding of IHSS following a huge rally conducted by homecare workers and IHSS consumers.

OCTOBER 1989–DECEMBER 1989
Local 434B wins dues check-off for members.

The union campaigns against arbitrary cuts in IHSS consumers' hours and demands that a copy of the notification of any cuts be sent to homecare providers as well.

1990s

JANUARY 1990
The union begins a series of meetings with county officials to seek improvements to the IHSS reassessment and appeals system. Governor Deukmejian announces his intention to cut $71.1 million from the 1990 IHSS budget.

Richard Riordan, mayor of Los Angeles, recognizes Claudia Johnson, the first president of the local. Mrs. Johnson recently passed away.

JUNE 1990
Governor Deukmejian withholds home-care workers' paychecks. Community groups and legislators join Local 434B for rallies and demonstrations; demonstrators demand the release of the paychecks. The governor concedes and paychecks are released July 1, 1990.

Members at the Sacramento rally in February 2009.

AUGUST–NOVEMBER 1990
Over 5,000 members are recruited within three

months; membership reaches a total of 7,149 by the end of November.

MARCH–APRIL 1991
Local 434B meets with Assemblywoman Gwen Moore, who pledges to fight for homecare workers' rights and agrees to sponsor the Public Authority bill.

Local 434B takes its fight to Sacramento to lobby politicians on various issues affecting homecare workers.

MAY 1991
The union participates in a demonstration at the Los Angeles County Board of Supervisors, protesting the cuts in the county's IHSS budget, including staffing cuts in various IHSS offices. The pressure is successful and prevents any cuts in the IHSS staff.

"There were times when the groups went to the Board of Supervisors meeting unscheduled and made presentations. There were groups that did lobbying by going to individual supervisors and working early on with Kenny Hahn, who was certainly a yes person on the Board of Supervisors who helped immensely. At the city level the mayor showed great interest. I thought the major funding would be left to the Board of Supervisors because the mayor at times had Bill Elkins on his staff to sort of examine and see what could be done. So as the movement spread to the larger community, the media began to push it, and then organizations began to push homecare."

— Rev. Cecil Murray, former pastor of the First African Methodist Episcopal (FAME) Church and chair of Christian Ethics in the School of Religion at the University of Southern California

AUGUST 1991
Over 1,600 timesheets are lost in one of the IHSS offices. Local 434B protests this incident before the Los Angeles County Board of Supervisors until the supervisors order that providers be paid as soon as possible.

NOVEMBER 1991
Local 434B grows to over 15,000 members.

MAY 1992
Homecare workers testify at the Industrial Welfare Commission to increase the minimum wage. Local 434B joins in the fight to increase the minimum wage in California.

JUNE 1992
Governor Pete Wilson threatens to cut IHSS by $82 million and proposes a 20 percent cut in IHSS hours with no appeal rights. Local 434B, its allies, and members from the senior and disability communities hold a series of demonstrations, rallies, and letter-writing campaigns to protest the governor's cuts.

"I got involved early on. Getting to know Ophelia McFadden and some of the homecare workers themselves made it clear these were people who worked the hardest with the least recognition. I knew that it was extremely important that they be organized so that they could get fair wages and benefits."

— Gwen Moore, member of the California State Assembly

Assemblywoman Gwen Moore submits the Personal Care Option Bill, which would allow a portion of the federal Medi-Cal funds to subsidize a portion of IHSS so that cuts will no longer be necessary.

AUGUST 1992
Federal District Judge David Levi overturns a ruling protecting homecare workers from receiving IOUs issued by the state.

After receiving IOUs for over two months, Local 434B, along with other advocates, files a lawsuit to compel the state to release homecare paychecks. Homecare workers receive their paychecks within a week and a half.

Beatriz Hernandez and Claudia Johnson.

SEPTEMBER 1992

Governor Pete Wilson signs the budget. Demonstrations and intense lobbying efforts prove effective: IHSS is cut by only 12 percent and appeal rights are left intact, effective October 1, 1992. Local 434B launches a know-your-rights campaign for homecare workers and clients and disseminates information on how to appeal the cut.

Governor Wilson signs the Personal Care Option Bill, AB 1773, sponsored by Assemblywoman Gwen Moore.

NOVEMBER 1992

Local 434B and members from the senior and disability communities launch a campaign to fast-track the Personal Care Option Bill so that the 12 percent cut can be restored as soon as possible.

Local 434B participates in building a county-wide coalition in support of establishing the Public Authority as the employer of record for homecare workers. Over one hundred homecare workers and consumers attend the first joint union meeting.

SEIU member registers voters.

MARCH 1993

Supervisor Deane Dana introduces a motion requesting the restoration of the 12 percent cut and the establishment of a task force to review methods to improve the IHSS delivery model. The board unanimously adopts the motion.

APRIL 1993

IHSS workers, consumer advocates, and Local 434B successfully win restoration of full IHSS funding.

MAY 1993–1995

Extensive member training on political action mobilizes union members. On the heels of the IHSS victory, homecare workers increase outreach to new members and consumer coalition organizations to strengthen their power and to focus it on the passage of legislation that would increase the minimum wage for Californians.

Rev. James Lawson speaks at a rally for a fair contract in 2004.

MARCH 1996

Local 434B gathers over 80,000 signatures and puts Proposition 210 on the ballot. The initiative would increase the California minimum wage from $4.25 to $5.15 per hour.

JULY 1997
Local 434B takes thousands of late IHSS checks to the IHSS office in protest.

SEPTEMBER 1997
The Los Angeles County Board of Supervisors votes unanimously to establish a Public Authority in Los Angeles County and calls for the state to pay its fair share in funding the IHSS program.

MARCH 1998
Local 434B helps defeat California Proposition 226, the anti-union initiative promoted by right-wing forces and a section of big business. If passed, the law would have silenced workers and ultimately targeted the democratic rights of the working class.

Homecare workers in training.

NOVEMBER 1998
Local 434B submits 10,300 membership cards demanding an election for union recognition.

Governor Davis & State Legislators:
Invest in quality homecare this year!

Early homecare campaign leaflet urging the California Legislature to increase funding for In Home Support Services to consumers, about 1995.

FEBRUARY 1999
Local 434B wins union recognition for 74,000 homecare workers in Los Angeles County (16,000 voted yes; 1,900 voted no). It is "the largest union victory in the United States for over half a century," according to *The New York Times*.[1]

Victory for homecare workers.

AUGUST 1999
Los Angeles County homecare workers vote 26,000 to 260 to award Local 434B its first union contract for 74,000 homecare workers in Los Angeles County. The contract increases wages by $.50, from $5.75 to $6.25 per hour.

2000s

MAY 2000
After twelve weeks of campaigning, marching, rallying, letter writing, vigils, and erecting a tent city, homecare workers are successful in winning a wage increase of $1.00 per hour.

"My goal was to help aging Californians remain in their homes and live their lives with dignity. Homecare workers who come to the houses of the elderly were the reason that tens of thousands of Californians could remain independent. Without the invaluable help of homecare workers, many seniors would have been institutionalized. I am grateful to the Legislature for working with my Administration to provide homecare workers with the skills and training to allow our seniors to live with dignity.

— Governor Gray Davis (Ret)

Governor Davis signs AB 1682, legislation supported by Local 434B homecare workers. AB 1682 requires all California counties with 500 or more IHSS cases to "act as or establish an employer-of-record" for IHSS homecare workers by January 2003. Although the law maintains the consumers' right to hire, train, supervise, or fire their homecare workers, AB 1682 creates a new entity in each threshold county—the IHSS Public Authority—to serve as the point where IHSS consumers and providers come together for improved services.

The union also supports the governor's Aging with Dignity initiative, which allocates over $100 million in state funds to increase homecare workers' wages to $7.50 per hour and provide health insurance. The proposal also calls for wages to be raised to $11.50 by fiscal year 2004–05.

The passage of AB 515 enables Local 434B to receive access to a list of homecare workers in the state.

Assemblyman Mark Ridley Thomas speaks at a Homecare Workers' Rally, 2002.

AUGUST 2000
Homecare Worker Training Center classes begin.

SEPTEMBER 2000
Local 434B homecare workers win a $.50 wage increase for all homecare workers in Los Angeles County, to be implemented in November.

Los Angeles Mayor Antonio Villaraigosa shakes Maggie Beldon's hand, about 2005.

MARCH 2001
Local 434B homecare workers win health care benefits for all homecare workers who work 112 hours or more each month.

NOVEMBER 2001
Local 434B provides dental benefits for all Los Angeles County homecare workers.

APRIL 2002
The Homecare Protection Act is filed, with 386,000 signatures turned in.

Homecare consumers demonstrate to protect the homecare program against budget cuts, 2005.

MAY 2002
Homecare workers return to Sacramento to lobby against budget cuts to the IHSS program.

JUNE 2002
Local 434B wins union recognition for almost 11,000 homecare workers in San Bernardino County. It is the highest homecare voter turnout in the state.

AUGUST 2002
Homecare workers conduct a series of "We Need a Raise" rallies for increased wages and health benefits.

OCTOBER 2002
Local 434B homecare workers win the highest wage increase ever for all homecare workers, from $6.75 to $7.50 per hour. Homecare workers immediately begin working to reduce the minimum number of hours a provider has to work to qualify for health care benefits, from 112 hours to 80 hours per month.

Homecare organizing leaders. From left: Verdia Daniels, Beatriz Hernandez, Esperanza de Anda, Addie Parson, Maria Rodriguez, and Merry Simmons, Los Angeles Convention Center, 2000.

An SEIU Local 434 Homeworkers United demonstration.

JANUARY 2003
Thousands of SEIU Local 434B workers unite to create the Long Term Care Action Team (LTCAT). This diverse team of activists is responsible for holding local and statewide officials accountable to the IHSS program.

In their first contract, San Bernardino County homecare workers win a 20 percent wage increase to $8.50 per hour, including health care benefits for all 12,000 workers.

SEPTEMBER 2003
Tyrone Freeman revives Dr. Martin Luther King's Poor People's Campaign to address poverty and injustice in underserved communities. The broad coalition includes community, labor, and civil rights groups.

Local 434B's membership wins expanded health care coverage that will include 25,000 Los Angeles County homecare workers.

DECEMBER 2003
Governor Arnold Schwarzenegger proposes severe state budget cuts for fiscal year 2004–05 that would eliminate the IHSS Residual Program, reduce IHSS worker wages, repeal IHSS health benefits, and rescind the Nursing Home Wage Adjustment Rate Program.

JANUARY 2004
Local 434B helps to lead the Fight Back Campaign. This aggressive, nine-month statewide effort unites and mobilizes thousands of workers, consumers, and coalition partners into political action in protest of the budget cuts.

JULY 2004
Months of coordinated candlelight vigils, rallies, press conferences, lobby visits, phone calls, and letter-writing and media campaigns persuade the governor to withdraw his proposed cuts. Long-term care workers save and protect the IHSS program, the IHSS structure, and secured funding for nursing homes.

"We live in a society where people are poor and getting older and more ill by the day with no family or support system. It's a sad commentary on society. When you look at someone eighty to eighty-five years old, they can't fight for themselves. But that is what the home workers did. They fought for the people who didn't have a voice, the elderly and the sick. I think about myself being in that situation."

— Ophelia McFadden, union founder

AUGUST 2004

A federal waiver, Independence Plus, is approved to safeguard long-term care. The waiver delivers $340 million annually for five years to help California meet the needs of its aging population and its most vulnerable residents, expanding Medi-Cal health care coverage to include those receiving in-home care services through IHSS.

OCTOBER 2004

Los Angeles homecare workers win a wage increase from $7.50 to $8.10 per hour.
Homecare workers influence the passage and implementation of the Direct Deposit Bill, AB1470. The bill allows workers to have their wages deposited directly into their bank accounts.

DECEMBER 2004

Governor Arnold Schwarzenegger proposes severe state budget cuts for the second year in a row. The cuts would reduce IHSS worker wages to $6.75 per hour and hurt provider benefits.

JANUARY 2005

Local 434B begins work on a second statewide strategic campaign to fight the governor's proposed budget cuts to homecare services.

Homecare workers throughout Southern California begin hosting "Community Coffee" meetings. These informal gatherings in the homes of homecare workers provide support and connect communities of homecare workers to the issues that affect their lives and their communities.

MAY 2005

SEIU 434b leaders and Andy Stern, president of SEIU International, lead a massive rally to protest state budget cuts to homecare services.

JUNE 2005

Governor Schwarzenegger calls a special election for November 8, 2005. On the ballet are two corporate-sponsored initiatives—Propositions 75 and 76—that seek to silence the voices of homecare workers and deny union security to hundreds of thousands of public service employees.

Local 434B, along with the American Federation of State, County, and Municipal Employees (AFSCME), United Domestic Workers, engage in a statewide effort to improve and protect the IHSS program by launching the Uniting All California Homecare Workers Campaign.

JULY 2005

As a result of the statewide effort to protect homecare services, the governor announces that there will be no cuts. Over 105,000 Los Angeles homecare workers win a second IHSS contract that secures essential benefits and resources.

In their continuous effort to protect IHSS and its workers, Local 434B and SEIU International begin coordinating the efforts to unite homecare workers in several additional counties in California. SEIU Local 434B files petitions for representation elections in twenty-four counties for homecare workers.

SEPTEMBER 2005

SEIU International, SEIU Local 434B, and AFSCME sign an agreement to form the California United Homecare Workers (CUHW), a provisional union to work in partnership to represent and win contracts for the workers in all California counties that are without a contract. The CUHW union consists of twenty-five counties with close to 40,000 workers.

OCTOBER 2005

Local 434B successfully secures a second wage increase in less than one year for over 105,000 homecare workers in Los Angeles. Their pay increases from $8.10 to $8.45 per hour.

Senator Alex Padilla with SEIU 434B homecare workers in 2006.

NOVEMBER 2005

Homecare workers, their consumers, and hundreds of thousands of public employees across the state help to successfully defeat the governor's anti-union propositions in the special election.

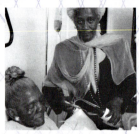

This homecare worker and her consumer were featured in SEIU's "Respect: We Deserve It" campaign to highlight the need for fair wages and benefits in the homecare industry.

DECEMBER 2005

SEIU International and AFSCME finalize the provisional bylaws that create the structure of CUHW and recognize Tyrone Freeman as the president. The CUHW has jurisdiction over 170,000 homecare workers in California.

The CUHW moves forward with contract negotiations with a letter and a survey on bargaining priorities sent to homecare workers in eleven northern California counties.

UNITED LONG-TERM CARE WORKERS' UNION

The logo for ULTCW.

OCTOBER 2006

SEIU 434B changes its name to SEIU 6434 United Long-Term Care Workers' Union and consolidates nine homecare workers locals into three. This restructuring, which is approved by homecare members across the state, increases industry focus and strengthens homecare workers' ability to win.

Homecare workers show labor movement solidarity by participating in a political action event sponsored by the Los Angeles County Federation of Labor, about 2005.

JULY 2007

SEIU 6434 membership surpasses 150,000, creating the largest union in the history of homecare organizing.

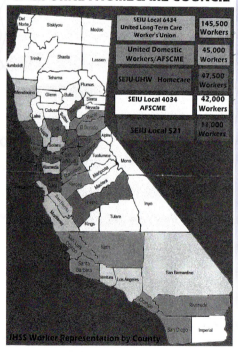

Map of California Homecare Council

Note

1. Steven Greenhouse, "In Biggest Drive Since 1937, Union Gains A Victory," The New York Times, 26 Feb. 1999, "Health," 1.